1. The Doctor and Christian Marriage

The Doctor and Christian Marriage

The Doctor and Christian Marriage

H.P. Dunn, MD

ALBA · HOUSE NEW · YORK

SOCIETY OF ST. PAUL, 2187 VICTORY BLVD., STATEN ISLAND, NY 10314

Library of Congress Cataloging-in-Publication Data

Dunn, H. P.
    The doctor and Christian marriage / by H.P. Dunn.
        p.   cm.
    Includes bibliographical references.
    ISBN 0-8189-0642-1
    1. Sex in marriage.   2. Contraception — Religious aspects —
Christianity.   3. Human reproductive technology — Religious
aspects — Christianity.   4. Marriage — Religious aspects —
Christianity.   I. Title.
    RG137.D86   1992   92-15244
    613.9'4 — dc20   CIP

Designed, printed and bound in the United States of
America by the Fathers and Brothers of the
Society of St. Paul, 2187 Victory Boulevard,
Staten Island, New York 10314, as part of their
communications apostolate.

PRINTING INFORMATION:

Current Printing - first digit   1   2   3   4   5   6   7   8   9   10   11   12

Year of Current Printing - first year shown
    1992   1993   1994   1995   1996   1997   1998   1999

To women —
source of life and laughter,
of love and loveliness.

But not forgetting the men —
strong, silent and faithful.

Table of Contents

MARRIAGE AND THE NATURAL LAW

THE title of this book is inaccurate — but only because of the constraints of space. It should really read: "The Doctor and Christian, Jewish, Moslem, Buddhist, Hindu, Humanist, etc., Marriage" because it aims to portray natural marriage for natural men and women, something that has been unchanged since the beginning because it is part of God's plan for the whole human race.

Imagine we were living in the centuries before Christ, say, at the time of Hippocrates (d. 377 BC), who is historically acclaimed as "The Father of Medicine." We could conduct our married lives and our medical practices in exactly the same way then as we do today because the principles are unchanging. Our motto in life, as in medicine, would always be: *Caritas et justitia* (love and justice), a noble and unfailing formula. Christ did not change any moral standards. He merely confirmed the Law and the prophets. Even in His strict teaching on divorce, He said that from the beginning divorce was wrong in essence and it always would be.

Similarly the Christian Church does not introduce any new standards for marriage, but simply confirms or elucidates the teachings of Christ. The principles set out here are those taught by the Roman Catholic Church, but in fact they were held by nearly all Christian denominations up till the present century.

PERSONAL APOLOGIA

As a practicing obstetrician and gynecologist for 40 years, I have been closely involved with marriage, sex and childbearing. Now that I have retired I can speak more freely without the suspicion of "advertising." I have Fellowships of: the Royal College of Surgeons (England); the Royal College of Obstetricians and Gynaecologists (England); the Royal Australian College of Surgeons; and the Royal New Zealand College of Obstetricians and Gynaecologists.

I have delivered some 15,000 babies, either personally or, in a few cases, sharing their care with colleagues. These were made up of: 4,600 private patients of whom I have an accurate clinical analysis; almost 2,000 unmarried mothers in the Home of Compassion; about 5,000 in the Mater Maternity Hospital clinic; and the rest during 40 years on the staffs of various public hospitals in England and New Zealand. This large number of children is equivalent to the population of a small town. Besides these there was at least an equal number of gynecological patients.

If each obstetric patient had an average of three vaginal examinations during pregnancy, four during labor and two in the postpartum and postnatal visits; and if the gynecological patients had three checks, this adds up to an enormous number of pelvic examinations. These figures are quoted to show that the writer has at least a passing acquaintance with the reproductive system.

Another interesting feature of my work in obstetrics and gynecology is that in all my years in the specialty I never prescribed contraception and never performed sterilization or abortion. It was an honor to be, like Christ, "a sign of contradiction." If these three elements of the antinatalist triad are really essential to good medical practice, then my patients should have shown up higher gynecological, maternal and perinatal mortality rates. This evidence is completely lacking. What it does show is a complete vindication for physiological, or "natural," living according to the design of the Creator. This is particularly true in the area of sexuality and of obstetrics.

One of the intangible benefits of trying to lead an ethical professional life is revealed when the occasional patient will say, "I know I can trust you." This should be taken as a tribute not to the individual doctor but to the professional code that until recently all doctors used to live by, enlightened by Christ and by that paradigm of the good pagan, Hippocrates.

It is obvious therefore that I write as a person who has had by virtue of his daily work a certain experience of marriage, sexuality and child-bearing. Hundreds of doctors have written similar books — why write another one? Because the great majority of the publications now available present a picture of sexuality that is erroneous, their principles are misguided, and therefore they are likely to do harm to the marriages of unsophisticated readers.

A DIFFERENT SEX EDUCATION

If she finds herself pregnant, your average teenager says tearfully: "My Mother never told me anything." For one thing, this statement completely ignores the circumstances that led up to her pregnancy, such as: drink, drugs, exposure to pornography, lack of modesty, the vulgarity that would allow intercourse with a virtual stranger. For another, she does not recognize that Mother has been giving her an unspoken lesson in sexuality over many years, an unobtrusive demonstration of how to live with love, tenderness, fidelity, refinement and spirituality.

People behave in the marital bed much the same way that they do during the working day, with a modicum of passion added. A person who is uncouth, ruthless or selfish at work will be exactly the same in sex. If a woman wants a gentle and considerate lover, she must first find a gentle man. And your true gentleman is the fruit of years of genuine spirituality.

In the sphere of family and social education, why should sex be treated differently from any other serious subject? Your average parent tries with indifferent success to inculcate some elegance and refinement in table manners but he is rarely so pompous as to state: "Thou shalt not rob banks"; or "Thou shalt not go in for drug addiction or alcoholism"; or "Thou shalt not embezzle the petty cash"; or "Thou shalt not vote Labour." But that does not mean that he has neglected his duties to his children. The lessons have been there over the years but not articulated. What parents hope for as they sink wearily into their graves is that the boys will have grown into Christian gentlemen and the girls into genuine ladies. There is no guarantee of success, but all that God asks of them is to do their best.

THEN WHY THIS BOOK?

If sex education is not the panacea that so many people imagine, why write an educational tome? It must be admitted that there are a few minor problems that young couples might not advert to which can easily be remedied. But in the broad field of sexuality there are many popular concepts that are destructive of married love and harmful to society. My aim is to clarify these.

The justification for this book and for its style of presentation is provided by an impeccable authority. Pope Pius XI (1930) in his great encyclical, *Casti Connubii*, stated (n. 105):

". . . it is indeed of the utmost importance that the faithful should be well instructed concerning matrimony both by word of mouth and by the written word, not cursorily but often and fully, by plain and weighty arguments, so that these truths will strike the intellect and be deeply engraved on their hearts."

As these matters are almost never taught from the pulpit, it remains for the doctor to do his feeble best. As the popular and available books are completely lacking in refinement and in moral principles, and as the religious ones are often vague and sentimental, the only way to remedy the situation and offer sound guidance to young couples is to write a book myself. Hence this *magnum opus*.

The Doctor and Christian Marriage

CHAPTER 1

Love and Marriage

WHAT is love? The most fundamental aspects of life are the most difficult to analyze and explain, even though everyone has experienced the reality of love. A man without love is already a monster. Love has many facets: *philia* is true disinterested love for mankind; *agape* means brotherly love as in a family or church; *storge* is natural affection, usually that of parents for children; *eros* implies the sentiments and emotions that lead on to sexual love. In human affairs there is usually an admixture of some or all of these aspects.

How do you know when you are "in love"? The mysterious alchemy which the Creator has instilled into human beings produces a turmoil of reactions in mind and body that can confuse the wisest man. Contrary to popular opinion, novels and the entertainment media, young people often experience pure disinterested love without erotic overtones. The pernicious influence of these opinion formers is such that the young are led to believe that there must be something wrong with them if they do not rush into a sexual relationship with every new friend.

If you are in love you have a feeling of warmth, excitement and good will. Your whole thoughts are centered on the beloved, you think of her constantly and long to be with her. In her presence you find contentment and peace, and you think only of what will make her happy.

But the diagnosis of this happy state is often difficult for inexperienced young people. Emotional assessments are often faulty. At the risk of being regarded as a romantic iconoclast I would suggest that the couple take the advice of reliable older people, preferably the parents. This sounds like a "counsel of perfection," but it would save many young lovers from making disastrous marital mistakes.

Love is one of the three theological virtues — "there remain faith, hope and love, but the greatest of these is love." (1 Corinthians 13:13) The love of God for mankind is an inexplicable mystery — "for God so loved the world that He gave His only begotten Son. . . ." (John 3:16) When asked what were the greatest Commandments, Christ answered in terms of love — first, love God; and the second is a corollary of this, love your neighbor.

With his special literary genius St. Augustine (d. 430) wrote two famous loving sentences which find an echo in the hearts of human lovers. *"Fecisti nos ad te, et inquietum est cor nostrum, donec requiescat in te."* (Thou hast made us for Thyself, O God, and our heart knows no rest until it rests in Thee.) And, speaking of the Church which he had long abandoned until he returned to her at the age of 32, he said: *"Pulchritudo, tam antiqua et tam nova, sero te amavi!"* (O Beauty, so old and yet so new, too late have I loved thee.)

Another penitent, St. Paul, in his incomparable hymn to love did not define it but described its operation in our lives: "Love is patient and kind; love is not jealous or boastful; it is not arrogant or rude. Love does not insist on its own way; it is not irritable or resentful; it does not rejoice at wrong but rejoices in the right. Love bears all things, believes all things, hopes all things. Love never ends. . . ." (1 Corinthians 13:4-8)

Every marriage is capable of following St. Paul's prescription for a truly loving relationship, provided it has a spiritual basis and aims at perfect unselfishness. Without spirituality marriage risks becoming a sterile desert.

St. Bonaventure (d. 1274) described love as: *"Vita copulans amantem cum amato"* (a life which unites the lover with the beloved). St. Thomas Aquinas (also d. 1274) described the marriage partner as *"amicus maximus"* (your best friend).

A JEALOUS LOVE

These comments from the great saints and doctors of the Church reveal how the marriage union is a private and unique love which excludes all others. This exclusiveness will be stressed repeatedly. In the Old Testament, God is often presented as a jealous lover of Israel. The first

Commandment states: "I am the Lord your God . . . you shall not have other gods before me." (Exodus 20:2-3) This is not sordid jealousy but a simple statement that you cannot have more than one "best friend," more than one to adore.

CHOOSING A PARTNER

Girl-friend days are golden happy days. But it is an injustice to keep going steady with a girl for an indefinite time unless there is a reasonable prospect of engagement. This monopolizes her and removes her from circulation when other prospective partners might be available. Youth is a time to have many friends and no commitments.

Engagement is a golden time, too. The romantic picture is that of Miss World marrying Mr. Universe, but for most people it is a matter of plain Jane making do with dull Desmond. Beauty is fascinating and if you have it you realize that it is a bonus gift from God, but it is better to opt for enduring quality of mind, heart and spirit rather than good looks. The head should rule the heart. A too sentimental approach to marriage can lead to regrettable errors. The following have been reported in our local paper recently.

Psychologist-social worker weds rapist allocated to her care. Woman marries prisoner who murdered her husband last year. Man marries quadriplegic patient who is permanently on a respirator. Teacher marries man with no arms or legs (a congenital abnormality). Prison wedding one day before execution.

Some allowance must be made for prudence and the dignity of marriage itself. A common mistake is for a girl to marry an alcoholic, or a drug addict, or a compulsive gambler in the hope of reforming him through the power of love and of her own goodness. In the great majority of such cases the plan is doomed to fail and there are endless unhappy years ahead.

It is almost a law of Nature that "like marries like." This is the situation with the majority of marriages. If a patient turns out to be psychologically disturbed, her husband usually is a similar type. Some say that "opposites attract." This may be true of electricity and magnetism, but with human beings the reverse is the case.

When people speak of "mixed marriages" they think mainly of religious differences but there are many other disparities which must be considered in choosing a partner. Religious philosophy is one of the fundamentals of human existence and, if there is a split at this level of an intimately shared life, the marriage must suffer an otherwise avoidable stress.

Until recently the Catholic Church was strict in prohibiting mixed marriages, but since the Second Vatican Council (1962-65) the restrictions have been relaxed and now about half of all Catholic marriages are mixed.

ENGAGEMENT

Engagement is a happy and unique time in each person's life story. It should be neither too short ("Marry in haste, repent at leisure") nor too long. Every couple's circumstances differ, but as a general rule one month is too short and one year too long. There are plans to make, families to consider, money to be saved, accommodation to be found and a hundred other things.

It is essential to get in touch with the parish priest at an early stage of the planning. Too often a starry-eyed couple call on him and say, "We want to get married next Wednesday, we've got the caterers arranged and my mother is arriving from the States. . . ." This is both thoughtless and ill-mannered. Besides booking the church, the priest, the organist and a host of other services there must also be a civil licence, proof of baptism and other sacraments, and evidence of freedom to marry.

Even more important is the pre-marriage instructions which most dioceses now insist on. It may take six weeks to work through these classes which ensure that the couple know the sacramental nature of marriage, their rights and responsibilities, sexuality, licit methods of family limitation, budgeting and finance, child rearing, and other secondary matters.

I remember one class I was taking for the medical lecture some time ago. They were taken aback when I said: "If you think you are old enough to get married at 18, don't come weeping to me after a few months saying: 'I'm pregnant but I'm too young to have a baby!' You've got to make up your mind right now. If you're old enough for marriage you're old enough for the whole deal." I heard later that one teenage fiancée decided to postpone her nuptials.

COMMON DISASTERS

It is a regrettable fact of life that large numbers of engagements are conducted in a less than ideal fashion, mainly in the area of sexuality. This is a modern phenomenon which has been ushered in by the so-called "sexual revolution," which itself has been spawned by militant feminists. Only a generation ago the majority of brides and grooms were virgins; now only a minority are.

It is true that women have over the centuries suffered from discrimination in several areas, financial, social, educational, political — but Women's Lib. tried to free them from their biology and their fundamental nature. It was an impossible task, foolish and shortsighted. The Women's Lib. priestesses regarded fertility, the hated womb and marriages as millstone around female necks and aimed to free women from all of them.

They abolished fertility by providing contraception, sterilization and abortion for one and all. The cyclical bodily function was sidetracked by menstrual extraction; and, with marriage being declared an outdated thralldom, *de facto* common law unions became all the fashion. The aim was to provide sterile sex for everyone, endless vistas of freedom and pleasure. In the short term this had a certain appeal, but in the long term it has been disastrous.

The importance of all this for engaged couples is the risk that they will fall for the Women's Lib. propaganda and welcome premarital sex, either in an opportunist way or in a more regular *de facto* arrangement. This temptation must be resisted at all cost.

The anomaly of modern sexual practices is clarified if one considers the time relationships of many young friendships. It used to be the norm for the couple to meet, then they fell in love, then they got married, then they went on the honeymoon, then had sex and finally she became pregnant. The sequence of events nowadays is often: first they have sex, then she gets pregnant, then they have the honeymoon ("shacked up"), then (if she's lucky) they get married, and finally (lucky once again) they fall in love.

It is obvious that this is all back to front. The ideal to aim at in life is control of the sex instinct. This is one of the aims of Christian moral living. Abandoning control leads on to unhappiness and tragedy and slow atrophy of the spiritual life.

This is what Mother Teresa of Calcutta said to a group of young people. It is really advice on sex from a living saint:

"You are the future of family life. In that future you can make your life something beautiful for God, a pure love. That you love a girl and that you love a boy is beautiful but don't spoil it, don't destroy it. Keep it pure. Keep your heart virgin. Keep your love virgin so that on the day of your marriage you can give something beautiful to each other — the joy of pure love."

This is mainly an esthetic and pragmatic approach to the problem, appealing as far as it goes. But there is another consideration which is much more serious and fundamental: What is the nature of the intimate relationship between the two partners? It can be only one of three answers: normal sex within marriage; fornication; or adultery. Sexual liberationists must be forced to answer. The usual answer is: fornication. And fornication is a serious sin. It was explicitly condemned by Our Lord and by St. Paul and that should be the end of the matter, whatever the Family Planning Association may say.

Our Lord said: "It is from the heart that man's wicked designs come, his sins of murder, adultery, fornication, theft, perjury and blasphemy. It is these that make a man unclean." (Matthew 15:18-20)

The gentiles were told to "abstain from idolatry and from fornication." (Acts 15:20)

St. Paul wrote: "But your bodies are not meant for fornication, they are meant for the Lord. . . . Keep clear then of impurity. Any other sin a man commits leaves the body untouched but the fornicator is committing a crime against his own body. Surely you know that your bodies are the shrines of the Holy Spirit who dwells in you." (1 Corinthians 6:13, 19)

Surely these authoritative teachings should be clear enough but in this mixed-up modern world there are hundreds of leading Catholic theologians who maintain that all the common sexual sins are permissible, provided that there is a loving relationship between the partners. This demonstrates the extent that the modernist heresy has infiltrated the Church over the past hundred years. It holds that there are no absolute standards in ethics; that the subjective assessment takes precedence over the objective (situation ethics); and therefore the end justifies the means.

If the theologians are confused, it is not surprising that the laity are even more so with the result that the incidence of sexual sin is almost as great among Catholics as among those with no religion. The situation is so bad that the Vatican in 1975 had to issue a *Declaration on Sexual Ethics* which simply restated the unchangeable fact that masturbation, premarital sex and homosexuality are wrong in every situation.

If a young couple make the common mistake and embark on sex before their final, definitive and irrevocable commitment in marriage, several unexpected sequelae begin to show up and impress themselves on their consciousness.

The relationship often becomes soured as the attractions of sex are outweighed by the realization that selfishness is a major factor in these demands. More damaging still, the truth hits home that the partner who initiated the original seduction, usually the man, is not committed to sex being confined exclusively to the married state and therefore he (or she) will be susceptible to extramarital temptations. Their trusting relationship is sabotaged right from the start. This may not apply to otherwise good young people who are deeply in love but, considering society as a whole, there is no doubt that fornication is just a training ground for later adultery.

Another serious consequence is that the spiritual life must suffer, the sacraments are neglected and the girl resents having lost her innocence — for what? Love instead of being fostered is killed and the common pattern is a sequence of one *de facto* relationship after another. Women come out of this self-destructive mess much worse than do men. A woman abandoned at 40 has little chance of marriage and children; but an unattached man at 40 still has the attractions of health and wealth. It should be obvious, as the world has known from the beginning, that the only real love and security are found in a pure and exclusive marriage as planned by the Creator for mankind.

How can the young avoid these all too common disasters? The first step is to have a vibrant spiritual life, that is, prayer, churchgoing, sacraments and penance. Only in this way can one gain protection from such seductive temptations. The next move is to strengthen the character and the will through regular self-denial and acceptance of hardship. It takes considerable courage to be different from the mob, especially when they are so vicious in their attacks on the shining virtue of purity. They should be recognized as allies of Satan, the great hater of innocence, even if they themselves do not realize who is their master. There are certain well-recognized sexual precipitating factors which should be avoided, namely, drink, drugs and pornography.

What if it is already too late? What if a young couple realize the mistake they have made by anticipating their final marriage vows and do not know what to do? The great message of Christ is that it is never too late. True, one can never retrieve lost innocence but one can regain lost purity and lost love. The sacraments were given for just this purpose. We have all lost something through sin of one form or another but He will wash us "whiter than snow" (Psalm 51:9) through the sacrament of Penance.

It is essential to discontinue the sexual activity until the wedding day and then look forward to a new life with a faithful partner and the blessing of children. I have observed that lovers in this abnormal situation usually make these moves instinctively before the wedding. They change over to abstinence and one partner moves out of the *de facto* home. It is not too difficult. Why did they not make this decision in the first place?

MARRIAGE

This happpy union to which young men and women are instinctively and inexorably attracted is described in the marriage ceremony as the sole remaining joy left to mankind since they lost everything in the Fall. It is a concession from God to give them an inkling of what life was like in the Garden of Eden. And most couples would agree that they sense this pristine feeling of being at one with an unsullied world, even if cares and worries inevitably follow.

Marriage is often described as "a great social institution," which gives the impression that man invented and developed it, but it is fundamentally God's institution. Therefore it is subject primarily to God's law and only secondarily to ecclesiastical and civil law. If the State finds itself at variance with God in marriage matters, it is the State which must change. For an example of this conflict we need look no further than divorce problems.

In recent years the startling increase in *de facto* unions and homosexuality has necessitated the defining of marriage and family so as to clarify things for Social Welfare organizations. The Family Rights Association (which I founded) defined the family as the legally married husband and wife and children, if any. It defined marriage as a contract and union that is heterosexual, monogamous and permanent. The State defined the family as any group of people living together.

The practical importance of this battle of words is that, by its laxist definition, the State financially supports *de facto* and homosexual unions and gives them a status that is equal to, and sometimes superior to, that of normal marriage. This is a disturbing injustice.

Vatican II defined marriage as a "community of love." It was designed by the Creator as the natural state for mankind to live in, to bring up children and to foster holiness, peace of mind and security. In that wonderful sentence in Genesis, God said: "It is not good for man to be alone." (2:18) It is often overlooked that marriage is a sacrament, that is, a means of grace — and that each partner has the obligation not only to love and care for the other but also to achieve the salvation of his/her soul.

St. Paul described marriage as "a great mystery." (Ephesians 5:32) Any attempt to write about it must therefore be inadequate, but the richness and complexity of God's design gradually unfolds for all sincere couples. St. Paul went on to compare marriage with the union of Christ and His Church. Love of its nature cannot be sterile and static; it must be fruitful and ever-expanding. In the human union it is fruitful of children, of grace and of ever-increasing love as in a chain reaction.

When Christ enters into His Church this divine union produces fountains of grace and innumerable saints. At the individual level He enters into each one of us through the Eucharist and generates further grace. The Eucharistic union was prefigured by the brilliant description of the marriage union in Genesis: "two in one flesh." These four small monosyllabic words describe perfectly this mysterious state.

Another interesting divine insight is that love can never be single. It must involve not one, not two but three persons — the one who loves, the one who is beloved and reflects back that love from a position of equal status, and finally the one who is the product of that love. For the first time in history Christ revealed to the world that there are three persons in God. The Council of Constantinople (381 A.D.) defined their relationship: the Holy Spirit "proceeds" from the (love of) the Father and the Son. The lightning flash of divine love between all three is instantaneous and eternal.

It should hardly be necessary to state that marriage is a heterosexaul relationship. This has been the situation since history began. To describe the union of active homosexuals as a "marriage" is a travesty and an insult to those in normal marriages. From a consideration of the anatomy and physiology of the reproductive organs, it can be deduced that mankind is designed for heterosexuality. The fact that sex can be undertaken in various perverse forms does not prove that these are "normal"; it proves only that perversion exists, as sophisticated observers have always known.

Once a couple have embarked on a heterosexual relationship they realize that they have set themselves apart from the rest of society forever. They have revealed to each other the most private physical and psychological depths, and it would be a treachery to go through the same shedding of defences with someone else. The manifestations of love in that secret garden make marriage essentially exclusive of all others, lifelong and monogamous. To have sex with another, whether premarital or extramarital in timing, is being unfaithful to the future or the present spouse. With their genius for *le mot juste* the Americans best describe adultery as "cheating." But, *sotto voce*, it must be admitted that Solomon, the wisest man in history, was polygamous to a fault — 700 wives and 300 concubines. The mind boggles.

Given the frailty of human beings and the sexually charged atmosphere of society, it is almost inevitable that infidelity will strike at many marriages sooner or later. The big risk time is after some 20 years of marriage when both partner are in their 40s. The wife shows signs of ageing earlier than the husband. He is still fit, successful in business and with a certain mature attraction — but he is suffering, perhaps unaware, from the common psychological fear of loss of sexual power. He forms an unwise attachment for a much younger woman who might be genuinely fond of him — but it cannot be denied that she can often see the financial advantages of such an investment in companionship. In a minority, but increasing number, of cases the boot is on the other foot and it is the wife who is unfaithful. Even more bizarre is for the husband to lose his wife to another woman, or the wife to lose her husband to another man.

DIVORCE

Divorce is the curse of modern society. Vatican II described it as "a plague." It has been with us since the beginning of recorded history, but the epidemic has probably never been so widespread as at present. The ratio of divorces to new marriages in any one year now lies between 1:2 and 1:4 in most Western countries. Not so long ago it was only 1:100. These figures represent the hidden tragedies of thousands of broken homes, spiritual disasters, disadvantaged children and the subversion of the status of marriage.

Every marriage service is vitiated by the unspoken existence of the escape clause of divorce. This is highlighted when the divorced make their solemn vows "until death" for the second and third time. Everyone has sympathy for the unfortunate spouse locked in an unhappy or unjust marriage and seeking an easy release from this situation, but acceptance of the principle of divorce in the first union obliges us to accept it also in the second, fourth or tenth divorce. The repeated marriages of Hollywood celebrities are an insult to genuine married people as they are obviously examples of serial polygamy. Of course, the essence of the debate is not about simple divorce but about divorce and the right to remarry. Sometimes good people must go through divorce to obtain certain civil and financial advantages, but remarriage is a more serious matter.

It is difficult to find anyone with whom one can discuss such a sensitive subject in an objective fashion, but I was once able to ask the question of an excellent Presbyterian friend.

"How can you justify divorce,"I asked, "in view of Christ's explicit rejection of it?"

"We feel it is the compassionate solution to the problem," he said. And that was considered sufficient justification.

It is just as well to review the New Testament teaching of Christ on this difficult and divisive subject.

"He said to them, 'For your hardness of heart Moses allowed you to divorce your wives, but from the beginning it was not so. And I say to you: whoever divorces his wife, except for unchastity, and marries another, commits adultery; and he who marries a divorced woman commits adultery.' " (Matthew 19:8-9)

A similar statement is found in another place in the same Gospel. (Matthew 5:32)

The qualifying phrase about unchastity presents a difficulty because Our Lord appears to be allowing an exception. The Eastern Churches permit divorce solely on the grounds of adultery. On the other hand, St. Mark and St. Luke present an absolute prohibition of divorce.

" 'What therefore God has joined together let not man put assunder.' And in the house the disciples asked him again about this matter. And he said to them, 'Whoever divorces his wife and marries another commits adultery against her; and if she divorces her husband and marries another she commits adultery.' " (Mark 10:9-12)

" 'Every man who divorces his wife and marries another commits adultery, and he who marries a woman divorced from her husband commits adultery.' " (Luke 16:18)

St. Paul confirms this teaching. "Accordingly, she will be called an adulteress if she lives with another man while her husband is alive. But if her husband dies she is free from that law, and if she marries another man she is not an adulteress." (Romans 7:3)

In another place he confirms that the teaching about divorce comes from Christ but he mentions the possibility of separation (without remarriage).

"To the married I give a charge, not I but the Lord, that the wife should not separate from her husband (but if she does, let her remain single or else be reconciled to her husband) — and that the husband should not divorce his wife." (1 Corinthians 7:10-11)

If any doubts still remain, they can be resolved by reference to tradition and the teaching authority of the magisterium. The Council of Trent (1545-63) was asked this very question and answered in the standard formula which makes an assertion through a double negative:

"If any man says that the Church is in error because it taught and still teaches, following the doctrine of the Gospels and the Apostles, that the bond of marriage cannot be dissolved because of adultery of one or both parties, let him be anathema."

It seems that in the modern world people rush into divorce too readily. There are, of course, reports of absurd and disgraceful couples who divorce after two or three days (!) of marriage, but the genuine cases of distress are those who have been married for some years and then have the marriage dissolved because of adultery, or alcoholism, or violence, or simply "falling out of love."

Of all the common sins, adultery is the most hurtful: the treachery, the insult of rejecting the true love and preferring another, the vulgarity of the sexual association, the realization that he is unable to control these instincts, the seriousness of the spiritual disaster, the destruction of dreams for the future. It is understandable if the wife (the more commonly affected partner) is so offended that she immediately withdraws all love and co-operation. She rushes off to see her lawyer and this professional usually advises an immediate divorce.

The truth is seldom revealed, but I know scores of patients who have bitterly regretted hurrying into divorce. They realize they should have held on and fought for their husbands and their families. There is no such thing as an unforgivable sin. If God can forgive, why should not we? It is possible to heal the hurt, even if it is not forgotten, as the years pass by. Sexual faults are evidence of human weakness and they have been with us since the world began. There is no such thing as a "double standard"; it is just that males are weaker in this area of life and more predatory.

Although our hearts go out to them in the sadness of their seemingly insoluble social dilemmas, Catholics who are divorced and remarried are in a tragic situation. The explanation for this cruel but self-induced blow is found in the words of Christ quoted above. Despite this, many official and parish organizations make pleas for the partners in such marriages to be admitted to the sacraments. If our pity allows us to analyze clearly the nature of the sexual relationship, this is obviously impossible. The only solution for them is the celibate life, a decision which calls for heroic courage. God in His mercy will look after them in ways we cannot know.

ANNULMENT

In recent times marriage annulment, once a rarity, has become so common as to be almost an ecclesiastical growth industry. In one New York diocese where the success rate of applications reached almost 90 percent, it became a scandal. "Catholic divorce" it was called. There is no doubt that many of these applicants could not possibly have fulfilled the requirements to justify annulment. It was probably a situation similar to that in the abortion industry where many doctors take the attitude that the request for abortion justifies the operation because it is evidence of mental stress or incapacity.

Despite all this, annulment is still a valid decision in civil as well as ecclesiastical courts. All that it states is that a true marriage has never existed and therefore the partners are free to enter upon another union as unmarried people. In either court, marriage legislation is very complex and essentially the province of professionals, but we amateurs can make a few simple statements based on common sense. State and church have the right to stipulate certain minimum requirements for marriage such as being over an arbitrary age (usually 16 for females and 18 for males) and free from psychological or communicable disease, such as AIDS.

The contract must be freely entered into with a clear understanding of the nature of marriage, and a genuine intention of both lifelong devotion and acceptance of childbearing. Pope Pius XII has stressed that if there was a definite decision to have no children, that would invalidate the marriage. Those who are simple-minded or psychologically immature are presumed not to understand the nature of the contract. This is the difficult matter to prove, especially many years after the wedding. It is the main source of dispute and scandal but, since the procedure is always confidential, any critics lack the essential information to make a contrary judgment.

In these days of worldwide movement of peoples it is becoming more common to encounter marriages of convenience for the sake of facilitating immigration. Such unions obviously do not have a genuine intention of love and permanency, and they should be ended by nullity rather than by divorce. It is usually the wives who are tricked into such situations.

The main cases in which a doctor may be called to give evidence about marriages in court, apart from psychiatric problems, are concerned with non-consummation. In both civil and church marriages, validity is not complete until there has been intercourse with penetration. The key observation is the state of the hymen, whether it is intact (*virgo intacta*) or ruptured. If it is intact, there are two alternative explanations: either the hymen is too tough or the orifice too small to allow penetration; or there is impotence (failure of erection) on the part of the husband.

In the recent past an intact hymen was a not uncommon finding but in the modern world it is rarely seen, thanks to tampon usage and promiscuity. When I had been in practice only a few years I was able to collect a series of 37 cases of hymeneal problems which I reported in the medical literature. [1]

The purpose of the article was to persuade colleagues to choose a method of treatment that was radical but certain to succeed. If the management was inadequate or too prolonged there was a risk of secondary (psychological) impotence. The choices available were: simple stretching of the hymen or nicking under anesthesia; daily use of graduated dilators; psychological retraining in sexuality; and plastic surgical enlargement of the introitus. The latter was my choice.

One patient had attended a psychiatrist for a year while he worked on the theory that her failure to achieve penetration was caused by an incorrect sexual attitude upstairs in her brain, but my opinion was that the whole problem lay in the downstairs department. I said to her: "I can fix that in five minutes" — which I did.

1. Dunn, H.P. "Unconsummated Marriage." *N.Z. Med. J.* (1958), *57*, 156.

2. The Doctor and Christian Marriage

One of the patients in my series later had a daughter-in-law who came complaining of exactly the same problem 23 years later. Fortunately she overcame the difficulty without an operation. Because of confidentiality I could reveal to neither party this unusual coincidence which I had to enjoy in isolation and secrecy.

Modern tribunal members tend to concentrate on the duress or immaturity factors and to ignore medical evidence, but sometimes it can be crucial.

Case Report

Some years ago an American lady came to see me with a menstrual problem, and an attempt at a vaginal examination revealed that the hymen was intact. She had presented herself as "Mrs. Doe" and stated that she was a divorcée. Her sad story gradually unfolded. She and her husband had had painful attempts at intercourse but thought that this was the norm for everyone, although she suspected that something was not quite right. Repeated frustration led to anger and a cooling of love. They went to the marriage tribunal of their city and were making some progress, but unfortunately the doctor she visited and the priest in charge both died within a month.

She and her husband were left up in the air. They drifted apart and after a couple of years he divorced her. She later tried to enter a convent, but as a divorcée she could not be accepted. He married another Catholic woman and had a couple of children; the whole family kept going to Mass but because of his divorced state the parents could not receive Holy Communion.

Everyone involved in this small human drama had suffered an injustice. The marriage should have been annulled on grounds of non-consummation; they should not have been labelled as divorced.

Setting things right took considerable persistence as neither the local bishop's secretary nor the chancellor of the American diocese was anxious to take up such a remote and contentious case, and even the patient lacked drive and keenness. Eventually, however, the two tribunals accepted my clinical evidence and the original marriage was annulled. The American husband, a *persona incognita* to me, had his second marriage blessed and validated, he and his wife returned to the sacraments, and the children benefited from being members of a united family.

THE WEDDING

This is a day of love and happiness and beauty and romance. Even a plain girl looks lovely as a smiling bride; and the ordinary man is like a knight in his wedding suit. There is no place for the second-rate or the meretricious — this is not to say that everything must be as expensive as possible but that the aim should be for good taste and dignity, qualities that are available to the poor as much as to the rich.

A wedding is a great family occasion, but if there are too many guests it gets out of hand. The upper limit should be about 100; if there are more than that, the bride and groom cannot possibly know them. About 50 is the ideal. It is quite impossible to include all relations and social contacts.

What to wear is a difficult decision. Nothing is more beautiful and romantic than a traditional bridal gown. For once the expense should be ignored. But a common mistake is for the bride's and bridesmaid's dresses to be too low cut in front and at the back; and for the train to be so long as to be an embarrassment.

If the bride already has a baby with her, or if it is public knowledge that she has been living *de facto* with the groom, she should not wear white. This serves only to annoy their friends and family. She should choose gold, pink, ivory or dove gray.

If, on the other hand, she has had a previous intimate relationship but that is not generally known, there is no need for her to make public intimation of the fact by eschewing white. That is her private business. Everyone entering marriage has some fault or other in the past; no-one is perfect. Should the engaged partners reveal all to each other? Definitely not, unless it is inevitable that the fact will be revealed in the future, for example from an abdomen ruined by striae (stretch marks), or a Caesarean scar.

The bridegroom and his escorts are well advised not to go in for bizarre outfits with frilly shirts that make them look like a Mexican band, or for traditional formal attire that would be appropriate for Derby Day at Ascot but does not sit comfortably on modern muscular young men.

A church wedding should be the norm because marriage is a sacrament and a religious occasion. A Registry Office is surely the most sordid way of pledging oneself to the beloved for life.

The ideal is to have a Nuptial Mass, the epitome of beauty and spirituality, a priceless gift available to all who ask for it. Regrettably, so many young people turn the gift down and opt for a truncated marriage service, apparently to oblige non-Catholic family or friends. It is like renouncing one's citizenship.

Now that the couple can choose their own readings and prayers and hymns, there is an unfortunate tendency to introduce secular works into this religious setting. There might be long paragraphs from "the Prophet" Gibran or some other guru; and songs from the latest pop group, such as "Help me to make it through the night"! When the words of these modern geniuses are analyzed dispassionately, they nearly always turn out to be sentimental drive, which has no place in a church. Surely there are sufficient richness in the Scriptures and in the official hymns, both ancient and modern.

The soaring cost of catering is causing a reassessment of traditional receptions. It is unfair that the father of the bride should have to bear all the cost, simply because of tradition. This arrangement is a hangover from the days when brides were accounted of little intrinsic value and had to bring a dowry into the marriage. In these more enlightened days of equality, both families should share the burden. In fact, the young couple would probably prefer to have the money and save on the reception. A better idea when she comes from a circumscribed parish is to invite everyone who cares to come, but to make the arrangement a B.Y.O., the traditional "ladies a plate, gentlemen a bottle (or two)." This makes everyone happy.

There is no need to serve the most expensive French champagne, as 90 percent of the guests would not be able to detect its quality. Providing a sparkling wine and a still white wine is sufficient for the whole reception. If spirits are offered the hard drinkers concentrate on them rather than on the bride and groom, with predictable results. The speeches and toasts are sometimes brilliant but the groom or the M.C.

must act to quash the embarrassing vulgarity that often mars these happy hours.

I must confess to an almost irrational antipathy towards photographers. They should be prohibited inside the church because, with their flashes and their very presence, they detract from the dignity of the marriage ceremony. Dressed in casual attire like gypsies, while all the congregation are in their "Sunday best," they invade the sanctuary even at the most sacred time of the Mass. Each lovely young bridesmaid must pose as she is signing the Register, which is now carelessly laid on the altar of sacrifice. Is it really necessary to have every moment of the ceremony documented? Is it worth the huge fees charged? Let them practice their arcane rites outside the church doors.

CHAPTER 2

Sexuality and Childbearing

"MALE and female He created them." (Genesis 1:27) This is the design of the Creator, therefore it must be good. Marriage is all about sex — but not quite all about sex. All marriages have to do without sex for a shorter or a longer time, but that does not mean it is an "optional extra." It merely implies that, while sex is of the essence in a marriage, it should be kept under control. If sex is not under control it can become a monster, as witness the "sexual revolution" which has brought with it an explosion of vice, infidelity, rape and violence. Whereas God's plan in sexuality leads to love, fidelity, peace and holiness.

As St. Paul said, marriage (and this includes sexuality) "is a great mystery" (Ephesians 5:32) which in a way is reminiscent of the union of Christ and His bride, the Church. The complexity of human love and reproduction is so wonderful as to defy analysis and the imagination. It is a test of faith to believe the words of the marriage service to the effect that, if we adhere to God's plan and avoid the common sexual sins, He will guarantee us "the greatest measure of happiness that is possible on this earth." I have seen this being achieved in innumerable good marriages.

ORGASM

Thousands of words have been written about this subject in magazines and books on sexology, but it would be fair to say that no-one really understands this interesting psycho-neurological reaction and therefore there is no unfailing formula for success. In modern medicine we still know very little about how the body works, even though some of the recent advances have been quite brilliant. Can anyone explain a simple phenomenon such as being ticklish? Why are some people susceptible and others not? We do not understand common problems such as dysmenorrhea or infertility. If we did, we could cure them all.

In the male, orgasm and ejaculation is almost invariable until advancing years begin to take their toll. From the viewpoint of reproduction and the perpetuation of the species, ejaculation (and therefore orgasm) is essential for the male but no such reaction is needed by the female. It seems that fertility is almost independent of orgasm, even if it is associated with some form of uterine contraction. The male role is to be active while the female, if not entirely passive, is somewhat less dramatic.

Nevertheless, we can point to some factors which facilitate orgasm and others which make it difficult to achieve. For optimum performance it is useful to recall the old saying: "The chaste wife makes the best lover." Many do not realize the profound truth of this observation and they may harbor an unspoken envy of the well-publicized nymphomaniacs who have sex unceasingly with a vast variety of so-called "lovers." In many cases they are quite frigid. In fact, it would be physically impossible to keep up this pace indefinitely. It is a sort of mania induced by abandoning decent standards of living.

In early marriage it takes some time to develop the orgasmic facility. In human sexual activity, husbands tend to be quick while wives are slower because it takes time for the specific physical reactions, such as production of cervical mucus discharge, to develop. This mucus is obviously Nature's lubrication to facilitate penetration without discomfort. Husbands must therefore learn to slow down and wives to speed up, but the psychological reactions are as important as the physical and they follow on gradually from private demonstrations of love and affection. Having intercourse is much more meaningful and serious for wives than for husbands because of the future implications of pregnancy and delivery.

The essence of sex is in giving. Each partner gives to the other the privilege of admission to this secret area of life where the deepest personal feelings are revealed. This requires complete trust and confidence, and it produces a feeling of security which can never be found by those who have multiple partners, either before or after marriage. The working rule therefore is not to embark on sex unless the other partner wishes it. It is not a matter of: "I want it, and I want it now. I demand my marriage rights." Such a marriage is already in peril. Love cannot flourish in these circumstances.

The husband must learn to defer ejaculation and prolong the act so as to allow the wife time to achieve the climax which is encouraged by this mutual giving. Sex should be undertaken mostly for the sake of the other partner, not for oneself.

Factors which militate against sexual satisfaction are: painful intercourse (see later); lack of decent privacy in the home; a too rapid performance on the part of the husband; any bizarre position for the act; an abnormal fear of pregnancy; coitus interruptus (withdrawal); oral contraception, if this causes reduced libido; use of other contraceptives, if these offend against her sensibilities; and lack of love or of mutual trust.

Aphrodisiacs are a complete waste of time for either sex. In the Orient there is a thriving trade in such things as powdered rhinoceros horn or deer velvet (young antlers) for failing potency. This sort of business is almost immoral in its delusion of simple people; it also has led to the virtual extinction of the poor hunted rhinos in Africa. Alcohol is popularly thought to relax the tense psyche or to facilitate the seduction. In practice it is more likely to produce a somnolent partner or one who is "crying drunk," or even "fighting drunk." As in many other activities such as fighting, shooting, flying, driving, the human being functions best when alert and fit.

Young couples should be warned against turning to pornography in the hope that this will improve their sexual performance and response. It is a project fraught with danger and it is likely to do more harm than good. The rationale behind it is persuasive — they hope the pornographic magazines or videos will have an erotic stimulus; and they think they will learn a few tips from the "professionals." But in this case it is important to realize that the professionals, however pretty or handsome they may be, are involved in perversion and there is nothing to learn from perverts.

The danger is that this type of material leads on to addiction, more often in the males than the females. Then the emphasis in the privacy of marriage turns to the erotic rather than giving pleasure to the other partner. Sensitive wives find these presentations distressing because most pornography is based on the degradation of women. The husband may be inclined to try out bizarre procedures which he would otherwise never know about, and this will be humiliating for the wife. Wives should never be maneuvered into the situation where they feel they must be competing with prostitutes in their sexual activities. In a certain number of marriages which break up in the 40s the explanation is that the husband, fearful of advancing age, has become hooked on pornography. Finally, viewing pornography is a sin against purity; it should be undertaken only by those with a professional duty, such as police or censors. Most people close their eyes to this unwelcome truth.

SOME DIFFICULTIES

For husbands the three main problems are impotence, premature ejaculation and failure of ejaculation. The last can be dismissed as mainly a feature of old age when the volume of semen becomes less and the ejaculatory mechanism gradually breaks down. There is no satisfactory treatment, apart from acceptance of the situation.

Impotence means a weak or failed erection so that penetration is impossible. Naturally it causes considerable frustration in both husband and wife. Erection is a complex hemodynamic phenomenon which is dependent on engorgement of the organ with blood. It is easily deranged by psychological, neurological or general health problems, or simply by getting older. It is therefore difficult to treat and too much reliance must not be placed on psychiatrists or general physicians.

The urologists have developed solid penile implants to stiffen up the organ; or even to blow it up by means of water-filled implants which are pumped up by hand. The whole idea in resorting to this ingenious surgery is simply pathetic. It is similar to old ladies having vaginal enlargment operations to meet the demands of their husbands. It turns what should be a loving encounter into a surgical stunt.

Recent advances in vascular surgery have been used in some impotence patients, either microsurgical reconstruction of the arteries or ligation of the veins to reduce leakage of the blood flow.

Another interesting attack on the blood supply of the inefficient penis is through papaverine injections which the patient gives to himself, right into the deep structure (corpora cavernosa) of the organ, whenever he wishes to have intercourse. Sometimes things do not work out quite as expected. The eager male either has a fit or simply goes to sleep. Occasionally the response is greater than anticipated — priapism (an erection which persists for some hours or days), and this requires a visit to the hospital to have the embarrassing phenomenon corrected. In medical practice it takes judgment, and sometimes courage, to know when to "leave well enough alone."

In younger men the main cause of the problem is psychological. If there is lack of confidence, repeated failures become self-defeating; but by the same token success builds on success. The main therapy is patience and encouragement on the part of the wife.

Impotence is a constant worry for the lecherous section of society who go in for frequent intercourse with a large number of partners. For them the treatment must be prolonged abstinence until the stimulus operates normally again. For the best results sex must be disciplined and under control. This is an unwelcome prescription for many people, but in passing it highlights one of the unrecognized benefits of the natural family planning system in which the partners have to abstain for a week or so during each monthly cycle. This enforced rest undoubtedly results in greater satisfaction when intercourse is resumed. It is just one more example of the complex genius of the Creator in this human activity.

In a similar way the ludicrous, but entertaining, anomaly of public nudism soon suffers from a blunting of its erotic appeal. For maximum effect nudity should be the extraordinary, not the ordinary, state of affairs. It is well recognized that a fair proportion of nudists are impotent. A little reflection confirms that this must necessarily be the case, otherwise they would not be able to get ahead with the serious things of life such as cooking and tennis. How embarrassing normality might be!

Many systemic illnesses, such as diabetes, affect potency and it is obvious that neurological degenerative conditions affecting the spinal cord or its nerve branches will have the same effect.

Some drugs have adverse effects on potency, one of the commonest examples being tablets taken for high blood pressure. The other main drug to implicate, even without going to see a doctor, is ethanol (alcohol). As they drift past middle age and into the executive class, many men imperceptibly move into a clinical state just short of overt alcoholism and they themselves are the last to make the diagnosis. The nightly routine becomes a few whiskies or gins and tonic and three or four glasses of wine with dinner, and at the same time a gradual reduction in potency. If they realize the nature of the problem, a Lenten abstinence from sex and drink will improve matters.

Shakespeare, that incomparable genius, recognized this clinical syndrome 400 years ago. "It [strong drink] provokes the desire, but it takes away the performance." (*Macbeth*, II, i, 11) And, referring to the effect of ageing on potency: "Strange that desire should for so many years outlive performance." (*2 Henry IV*, II, iv, 284)

How could this literary giant in a relatively short life (52 years) accumulate such a fund of social and clinical experience? He must have observed everything and forgotten nothing.

Premature ejaculation (*ejaculatio praecox*) afflicts all husbands at some time or another, but it is a problem only when it is habitual. As the name implies, there is ejaculation soon after penetration, and this prevents the wife from achieving her climax. This causes frustration and sometimes anger. With patience most cases solve themselves. The mechanism is similar to that controlling the bladder — and as everyone knows, some children take longer than others to establish this control and stop bedwetting. The current favored treatment is "the squeeze technique" (squeezing the end of the penis before penetration) but it strains credulity to accept that this will be very effective.

In the wife the three main sexual problems are: painful intercourse (dyspareunia), lack of libido (frigidity), and inability to achieve orgasm (anorgasmia).

It is easy to see how dyspareunia can cause distress in the marriage because it puts the wife off having intercourse. It is important to establish whether the pain is located at the entrance to the vagina (introital) or well down in the pelvis (deep) because the management is different in each case.

If the pain is introital, it is almost certain to be because of the tightness of the orifice in the hymen. If this opening is very small penetration may be impossible, but even if the hymen has been ruptured and penetration is achieved the rigidity of the tissues may make for pain. With patience and persistence the opening is gradually dilated and the pain disappears.

A simple remedy to assist in this process is for the wife to apply an ordinary domestic cream to this area before intercourse. There is no need to go down to the drugstore and solemnly purchase a tube of K-Y Jelly. The only reason doctors use this lubricant is that it is non-greasy and it does not persist on the skin for very long. And it is unwise to rush off to the doctor too early in the romantic drama. Sometimes a patient asks for an urgent appointment on a Monday morning; she has been married on Saturday and they "can't manage." The best advice is to "come back in two months." By that time most of the couples have solved their own difficulties; and moreover they have been protected from a knife-happy surgeon.

On the other hand, there are some wives who undoubtedly need an operation to enlarge the introitus. In one of my patients the introitus was impossibly rigid. She had the operation, conceived immediately and nine months later delivered a 10-pound baby without needing stitches.

Deep dyspareunia is quite a different, and usually a more serious, problem. The pain is felt only with deep penetration because the cause is within the pelvis itself. While in many cases the treatment is by hormones or antibiotics, a significant number need surgery. The following are possible causes of the pain: retroversion of the uterus which carries the ovaries backwards into the depths of the pelvis where they are pressed on during intercourse; endometriosis (bleeding into the pelvis at period time) causing a fixed retroversion; a simple ovarian cyst; pelvic infection, whether acute or chronic, involving the tubes or ovaries; an intrauterine contraceptive device; and a dozen other conditions. It is obvious, therefore, that if this type of deep dyspareunia persists, the wife should see a gynecologist.

Lack of libido, the absence of normal sexual feelings and desires, is a complex problem for which a simple cause or remedy is difficult to find. The most likely explanation is a psychological one, because we must assume that structure predicates function — in other words, if the anatomy is normal the physiological capability must be present. Psychiatrists usually link frigidity with unhappy sexual experiences or assaults during childhood, but this explanation remains unconvincing. Women's psychological toughness and resilience enables them to forget the past and recover from traumatic events, even war.

Husbands must realize that, unlike the male, the female reproductive system works in a cyclical fashion and therefore the pattern for wives is one of rest and activity. This incidentally is one of the unexpected benefits of the natural family planning system. Libido declines during illness, during pregnancy and after delivery, and also in the presence of serious social or family problems. This knowledge should stop some husbands from complaining in a childish way, "My wife doesn't love me any more." It might even save lives! The basis for this apparently preposterous statement is two cases reported some years ago in an Asian journal of obstetrics and gynecology. These Indian women returned home after hysterectomies, their husbands immediately resumed intercourse, ruptured the vault of the vagina and the patients died. If they had loved their wives more than they loved sex, these unfortunate women would not have lost their lives.

It is not generally realized that oral contraceptives affect libido adversely in many cases, probably through a hormonal effect. They also cause depression and irritability. The patient will say that after she discontinued the pills she felt that "a cloud had been lifted from my mind." It is impossible to prove, but the suspicion remains that the habitual mood change and the disinclination for sex must lead to marital conflict and even to divorce.

The ordinary pattern of life is for libido to decline gradually with the passing years, especially after menopause. In the nature of things, sexual capacity persists to a greater age in husbands than in wives. This sometimes is a cause of conflict, but husbands must accept this as a fact of life and be prepared to forgo satisfying their natural instincts. This is a real test of love, but if their habitual practice has been to undertake sex mainly for the sake of the other partner, the stress should not be too great. As the marriage ceremony said: "Sacrifice is always difficult and irksome but love will make it easy and perfect love will make it a joy." That is the ideal formula for happy sexuality.

If the orgasm proves to be elusive, no-one has a guaranteed remedy and therefore it is not a good policy to go from doctor to doctor seeking a solution. Common sense dictates that plenty of time should be taken over the act (but not to the extent that one of the partners falls asleep!) and awkward positions for intercourse should be abandoned. Sometimes a philosophy of acceptance is the only way to cope with sickness or the other crosses in life.

PREMARITAL EXAMINATION

Sometimes in an excess of zeal young couples feel impelled to go to the doctor to have a "check-up" before getting married so that they can offer themselves to each other in tip-top condition, well groomed and with rippling muscles like a race horse. In the case of the fiancée there is always the unspoken question about how she is going to "get on." That depends largely on the state of the hymen, but it is a question that must usually remain unanswered until the inescapable test of "trial and error."

For the average fit young couple, a medical Warrant of Fitness is quite unnecessary. It is similar to the routine health checks that are so fashionable among top business executives — a complete waste of time and money. It is true that some pathologies such as high blood pressure may be symptomless, but such cases are a small minority. While early diagnosis is valuable in some conditions, the humbling fact is that most illnesses progress in an inexorable fashion. Before embarking on this clinical voyage of discovery, the young couple should be clear in their minds about what will happen if some pathology is found. Are they going to postpone the wedding? Even cancel it?

Admittedly, some diseases should be revealed well in advance of the nuptials, such as the possibility of a familial genetic defect that might affect the children; a shortened expectation of life from, say, chronic kidney failure; being a practicing homosexual; and nowadays the fact of AIDS infection which will lead to the early death of both partners. (There have been numerous instances of AIDS patients knowingly, but secretly, infecting various sexual partners.)

A rare and interesting problem arises when the future husband has a history of previous mumps complicated by bilateral orchitis (inflammation and swelling of both testicles) — is he now sterile? If the testicles are quite small it is likely that no sperm cells are being produced, but in most cases potency (erection) and ejaculation of seminal fluid is normal. The average doctor will advise a masturbation specimen of semen for laboratory examination, a quick and easy answer to the question. The doctor with clear ethical principles will see that masturbation is illicit in all circumstances; but the spontaneous ejaculation during nocturnal emissions can be used to make the diagnosis. This is easy to do if the subject is given a glass microscope slide and coverglass to have available. But he might have to wait some time to complete the test.

As Pope Pius XII has pointed out, potency is essential for a valid marriage but fertility is not. That is, married partners have the right to intercourse but not necessarily to have children. There need be no guarantee of fertility. Therefore a marriage may be annulled if there is an inability to have intercourse, but not if there is sterility in one or the other partner.

CHILDBEARING

It cannot be stressed too often that childbearing is of the essence in marriage. It is not an optional extra that can be accepted or rejected as the spouses may wish. Sexuality within marriage is designed not only for love but also for life. It is impossible to get away from the simple fact that a species or a race that does not reproduce is doomed to extinction. As the next few decades will show, race suicide has already arrived — particularly in Western countries.

People sometimes wonder how many children they would have if they rejected family limitation altogether and tried to have as many babies as possible. The answer is provided by the Hutterite communities in the United States. They had their origin as a form of Anabaptist belief (rejection of infant baptism and reliance on baptism of the Holy Spirit) under Jacob Hutter (d. 1536). One of their tenets is literal acceptance of the words of Scripture, particularly the sentence in Genesis: "Increase and multiply and fill the earth." (1:28) They proceed to do this with great courage and more trust in Providence than is found among Catholics and other Christians. They therefore have large families but they do not suffer starvation or poverty.

Their family structure was described about 1955 in a fascinating monograph (which I regret I cannot trace) by an American author under the title; "Man's Capacity to Reproduce. The Demography of a Unique Population." The researcher found that the average family was 10.5 children and the range was from zero to 20. In almost every Western country at present the average family size is under 2.0 children — they "can't afford" any more. And the Chinese Government has instituted its absurd one-child family policy which is enforced by many cruel coercions, including forced abortion. It would be fairly safe to assume that there are no Hutterites in China.

The catastrophic fall in national birth rates since the introduction of the contraceptive pill in 1960 and the subsequent acceptance of the antinatalist philosophy has produced such small families that the next few decades will provide many interesting examples of demographic collapse. Large populations and vigorous immigration obscure the problem for many years but in small countries the crisis becomes startlingly obvious. This can be seen in Singapore, which is now pleading with its citizens to have more children because there are not enough young people for the work force or for defence. I was there about 1970 when their ruthless antinatalist policy was introduced. It should have been obvious to anyone with common sense that the present crisis would inevitably occur.

Now Japan has joined the list of countries seeking to increase the birth rate and the work force. Singapore has to import workers from Malaysia, and Japan from South Korea. Once again, this situation was completely predictable from the time in 1945, at the end of the Second World War, when Japan embarked on her contraception and abortion policies. Both Singapore and Japan were obsessed with their small size and high population density, and moreover they could see, but only in the short term, that having few children is a financial advantage. Almost too late, they have realized that there is no escape from the biological law which requires growth. If an organism or a society is not growing it is dying. There is no steady state in between. That is, ZPG (Zero Population Growth, where the birth rate and the death rate are permanently equal) is a demographic fiction, an impossibility, because it overlooks the inexorable ageing of the population. The citizens gradually pass out of the childbearing years into the dying age groups.

The latest country to wake up to "the impending demographic

catastrophe" is Italy, which is calling on the European Community to encourage Europe's women to have babies. "Europe could no longer exist without the dynamism of its youth, which is necessary for the innovative and creative spirit." Most wealthy European countries depend on immigrant workers from North Africa and the Mediterranean basin, and this has been a major factor in the spread of Islam.

The following figures are necessarily approximate, but they point out an important trend. In 1900 Europe accounted for 50 percent of the world population; in 1950 25 percent; in 1970 20 percent; and the projected figure for 2000 is 10 percent. For anyone who is grateful to Europe for its contribution to Western civilization, culture and religion, this trend is a tragedy. Since the antinatalist philosophy is at base a spiritual problem, only a spiritual renewal will remedy the situation. But it may already be too late. (Ref. *The Daily Telegraph* [London], Nov. 26, 1990.)

In 1974 at the World Population Congress in Bucharest I presented a paper entitled "Population Optimism," which was based on the ideas presented here, namely that the "population explosion" was hysterical and ZPG an absurdity. While I cannot claim that the audience found my presentation earth-shaking, at least I can state that all my demographic predictions have proved to be correct.

For simple replacement of the population to keep up with deaths most people assume that the average family size should be 2.0 children, or perhaps 2.1 or 2.2 to make up for human error. But these figures are too low, as has been shown by Professor Hubert Campbell of the Department of Medical Statistics, University of Wales. Campbell came to the conclusion that the figure should be over 2.4 children per family. His reasoning was based on the premise that every woman should leave behind her at least one fertile daughter. To achieve this, allowance must be made for the fact that at birth there is a 1.0 percent preponderance of boys; there is high infant death rate in the first year or two; about 10 percent of the girls will not marry; and of those who do some 10 percent will prove to be sterile. These figures add up to about 2.43 children per family. If this is the figure needed for replacement, that for healthy growth must be about 4.0. And if this was the average family, the range would be from zero to about 10.

Those who in an hysterical reaction dismiss these figures as preposterous, Victorian, unenlightened, etc. must face up to the fact of a lonely old age and the certain knowledge that at the end of their lives there might not be sufficient nurses, geriatric services, social welfare, superannuation or a sound economy. Even now there are millions of envious eyes just over the horizon looking towards weak and under-populated prizes. Will there be no-one left to defend the country?

In these supposedly educated and scientific days, the commonly accepted stance is to plan ahead for every aspect of life — career, finances, childbearing — but the results of this policy are often less than impressive. The cold, computer-like family planning usually ends up in the production of two undistinguished little mites.

Are the modern days of super-planning any better than "the bad old days" when people got married and just accepted the babies who came along? John Wesley (d. 1791) was the 15th of 19 children. If Mrs. Wesley had been living today, John would probably not have seen the light of day. His parents, the medical establishment and a disapproving society would have marshalled their destructive forces against this tiny genius and the world would have been the poorer for his nonexistence.

If I may be permitted a personal reminiscence, when we were married we "planned" with youthful enthusiasm on having six children. In the event we finished with seven. Conscious of the slight risks involved but sickened by the widespread rejection of children, we decided on having the last one when my wife was 45. We were re-warded with a beautiful and good (most of the time) little girl who gave us much joy and rejuvenated our lives. This sort of trusting in Providence is the modern test of faith.

Society's obsession with planning of individual pregnancies is the fruit of the Family Planning Association's persistent antinatalist pro-paganda. The parents do not seem to realize that their adverse re-sponses are really insulting to their offspring. When a new pregnancy is announced, the common and ill-mannered reaction is now: "Was it planned?" When the mother goes to book in with her obstetrician, more often than not he asks: "Is this a planned pregnancy?" Such a question is an impertinence and has no relevance to the doctor's primary duty which is to provide competent obstetric care. Every child has the right to believe that it was loved by its natural protectors from the beginning of its existence and throughout its life. And every parent has a duty to give it love and protection, however inconvenient or burdensome the pregnancy may be.

A moment's reflection will bring the realization that unwantedness is a fluctuating affliction. Most babies are unwanted in the first trimester of pregnancy, wanted in the next few asymptomatic months, unwanted during the last uncomfortable month and during labor, wanted and deliriously welcomed immediately after birth, unwanted when the breasts are engorged and painful, wanted during the enchanting years of infancy, unwanted as obnoxious teenagers and finally wanted as the parents pass into old age.

Yet the naive and faithless medical profession holds as an article of faith that if the young mother opines in the first few weeks of pregnancy that the child is unwanted, it is thereby condemned to a life of misery and rejection from which it can be rescued only by a cruel abortion. The whole ridiculous concept is accepted without the least scientific confirmation. If the mother at any stage changes her mind and feels that the child is wanted and loved and enjoyed, the theory must collapse.

When you have babies, it is not just for yourselves that you produce these treasures. It is also for their brothers and sisters, for their grandparents, for society and for God. It is common to see older couples passing into their 60s sadly with no grandchildren. Their own children are too mean, too concerned with money and careers, too sexually liberated to give their parents the great human joy and experience of seeing their grandchildren. In the whole of human history people have recognized the elemental satisfaction, as stated in the Old Testament, of "seeing your children's children to the second and third generation" but now many parents are condemned to loneliness in their declining years. In some cases, it is their own fault because they themselves when young rejected childbearing.

In recent years we see the spectacle of career women having their first babies about age 40. Having wasted their young years on professional pride, they suddenly realize that life is running out and they might miss the bus. Sadly many of them find that their natural fertility has disappeared, or they have been rendered sterile by prolonged contraception or repeated abortions.

The Second Vatican Council described marriage as "a community of love"; and, as to its fundamental purpose: "By their very nature, the institution of matrimony and conjugal love are ordained for the procreation and education of children, and find in them their ultimate crown." *(Gaudium et Spes,* no. 48) In appreciating the value of children the Fathers said: "Children are really the supreme gift of marriage and contribute substantially to the welfare of their parents." (ibid., no. 50)

This latter insight, which contradicts the current devaluing of children, shows clearly that they are an asset in the marriage rather than a liability. They provide the parents with a fundamental fulfillment because the passing on of life is the greatest achievement in every person's existence. The beauty, innocence and perfection of the little ones provide for the parents a living "art gallery" in every home. An unforeseen bonus is that the small children keep the father and mother so busy, even exhausted, that they have no energy for getting into mischief such as extramarital affairs! And in Third World countries where there are no social security schemes, the growing children are an insurance for the parents' old age.

As everyone knows, about 10 percent of marriages suffer the tragedy of involuntary sterility and, despite recent dramatic developments in gynecology, nothing can be done for the majority of these cases. Many of these courageous couples come to accept that this burden is part of God's plan for them, and they generously direct their lives towards adopting or fostering or other works of charity. An even worse tragedy is the voluntary sterility which has been embraced by so many couples in Western countries.

The obligation to have children is not oppressive or unrealistic. This recalls Jesus' famous statement which gives encouragement to every marriage: "Come to me, all who labor and are heavy laden, and I will give you rest. Take my yoke upon you, and learn from me; for I am gentle and lowly in heart, and you will find rest for your souls. For my yoke is easy, and my burden light." (Matthew 11:28-30)

We have a duty merely to have a reasonable number of children. For the average marriage this will be about four; for those in good circumstances, ten; but it should be stated quite plainly that for some it should be zero. God requires us to be prudent, not silly. What dilemmas would justify the zero option? If a war is raging; or if the country is suffering a famine; or in conditions of unrelieved poverty; or if there is a terminal illness in either spouse; and so on. The practical problem is: what method of family limitation to use.

Case Report

Of all my patients I can recall only a few who had a similar outlook to that of the Hutterites, but one more of acceptance than direct pursuit of a goal. One I particularly remember was a young pretty girl who had been married less than six months and was already pregnant. At the postnatal visit I asked her if she wanted any help in family limitation (which meant for us, of course, only natural family planning) and she said, No, she was not out to break records in having babies but she would do nothing active about it. Instead she would leave it up to Providence.

How charming! How refreshing! How delightfully normal, when almost every other woman wanted drugs or devices or operations that would keep children out of her life! "Kids are a curse." Or, they may be nice but you can have too much of them. After all, you've got to be sensible, you can't go on having babies one after another. You've got to be small-minded.

My friend and her husband eventually went on to have ten children. Not once did she come to me and make what is almost the standard introductory complaint about being pregnant yet again. With her refinement of instinct, she could see that this would be an insult to the defenceless unborn child who had not asked to be conceived. Her husband was in the middle income group and he had to do secondary jobs to keep things afloat but they lived a happy, faithful life in frugal comfort, and when the children grew up they nearly all went on to tertiary education of one form or another.

In fact I had hundreds of magnificent women as patients, some having no children because of sterility, others only small numbers while a few at the top end of the range had 8, 10, 12, even 15. To show how Providence provides, two of these women ended up as millionaires, thanks to unexpected inheritances. The times call for courage, and that courage is often rewarded.

HOW TO GET THROUGH PREGNANCY

The first difficulty is to find a pro-life doctor because of the legion of antinatalist practitioners who greet the new patient with the words: "Do you want it? Or do you want an abortion?" That illustrates what medicine has come to through abandoning the Hippocratic Oath and the Judeo-Christian Commandment, "You shall not kill." All this is hurtful to the young mother already caught up in the mystery and excitement of her first pregnancy. Fortunately the right-to-life organizations in larger communities usually have a list of "pro-life" doctors. This very description is a rebuke to a faithless profession.

Medicine and nursing serve the body and the mind, but they tend to forget about the spirit which is the most important element of all because it is immortal. By their nature women are more spiritually orientated than are men, and during pregnancy they become much more sensitive to this side of the personality. Childbearing is "procreation," a remarkable word that reminds them that they are co-operating with the Creator in bringing into being a new life and a new soul which already has an eternal destiny. It is therefore important to turn our thoughts to spiritual things and benefit from the prayers and blessings contained in our rich religious traditions.

From Psalm 22:

> *"Yes, it was you who took me from the womb,*
> *entrusted me to my mother's breast.*
> *To you I was committed from my birth,*
> *from my mother's womb you have been my God."*

From Psalm 127:

> *"Truly sons are a gift from the Lord,*
> *a blessing, the fruit of the womb.*
> *Indeed the sons of youth*
> *are like arrows in the hand of a warrior.*
> *O the happiness of the man*
> *who has filled his quiver with these arrows!*
> *He will have no cause for shame*
> *when he disputes with his foes in the gateways."*

From Psalm 139:

> *"For it was you who created my being,*
> *knit me together in my mother's womb.*
> *I thank you for the wonder of my being,*
> *for the wonders of all your creation.*
> *Already you knew my soul,*
> *my body held no secret from you*
> *when I was being fashioned in secret*
> *and moulded in the depths of the earth."*

Catholic mothers should not neglect to ask the priest for the Blessing of a Mother Before Childbirth.

In the Book of Common Prayer the Anglican (Episcopalian) Church has the ancient service of the Thanksgiving of Women after Childbirth, more commonly called the Churching of Women. With their unfailing talent for misinterpretation the feminists have perceived the Churching ceremony as an insult to women because it implies that prior to this they were regarded as in some way unclean. It happened to occur at about the six weeks stage when the normal lochial discharge was clearing up, hence they saw a similarity to the shunning of women in primitive tribes during menstruation. But this is obviously a ceremony of thanksgiving for the baby and the safe delivery.

> *"O Almighty God, we give thee humble thanks for that thou hast vouchsafed to deliver this woman thy servant from the great pain and peril of Childbirth. Grant, we beseech thee, most merciful Father, that she, through thy help, may both live faithfully and walk according to thy will in this life present; and also may be partaker of everlasting glory in the life to come; through Jesus Christ Our Lord. Amen."*

The Catholic Church has the Churching ceremony dating from the Council of Nicea (325 AD) where it is found among the "Arabic canons." It was presaged in the prescriptions of Leviticus; and, of course, in the Purification of the Blessed Virgin (Luke 2:22). Nowadays the ceremony is usually combined with the baptism of the baby.

In *So You're Pregnant,* my little book of practical advice about pregnancy and labor (Sydney: E.J. Dwyer, 1986) I quote a prayer for pregnant women contributed by Rev. Harry Emerson Fosdick, who achieved fame as the pastor of the prestigious Riverside Church in New York City. In *The Book of Prayers Compiled for Protestant Women* Fosdick wrote:

"When expecting a child — O God, giver of all good gifts, we praise and thank you for this gift of new life and the power to create life. Thou hast allowed us to join with thee in the creation of a human personality with an eternal soul. Prepare us in thine own way for the receiving of the child thou hast entrusted to us that it may be duly brought up in the light and love of thy Son, Jesus Christ our Lord. Amen."

The absence of a similar service for those who miscarry has been seized on by malcontents as another indication of the harshness of this "male-dominated" Church and its indifference to the sufferings of women. It is quite unreasonable to draw that conclusion. It is just that open discussion of miscarriages is a relatively modern cultural development to which the Church has not yet responded, if it ever will. In the past, women kept their feelings of grief and loss to themselves and were consoled by the conviction that the souls of these little ones were taken care of by "the universal salvific will of God."

Infant baptism has been the custom of Christians from the earliest times (in the first few centuries the majority of catechumens were, not surprisingly, adults) and it should not be neglected. Regrettably, in recent years many young parents either delay baptism for some unconscionable time or they leave their children to grow up unbaptized, which by definition means pagans. Sudden and unexpected death is a constant risk for infants. If it should occur, some of the neglectful parents will suffer bitter remorse. This is reminiscent of the Pelagian heresy of the 4th century, which denied the reality of Original Sin and took an over-optimistic attitude to the saving grace of God. It therefore discounted the urgency, even the necessity, of baptism.

Finally, childbearing should be appreciated for its spiritual benefits. In a remarkable phrase St. Paul said: "Woman will be saved through childbearing," presumably because she is co-operating with the Creator in her work of pro-creation, bringing into being souls for the Kingdom of God, both here and hereafter. There is no need for generous young people to rush off to Third World countries as missionaries. A much more pleasant and effective apostolate is to stay at home in comfort and have a few babies. As Pope Pius XII said to an Italian family society, having a large family is an expression of great courage and also of a lively faith in Providence. God will provide.

PREGNANCY AND DELIVERY

Like marriage in St. Paul's phrase, the delivery of a new baby is "a great mystery." However many times a patient, midwife or doctor experiences it, whether it be once or a thousand or ten thousand times, it is impossible to comprehend it fully. We are all involved in God's ongoing dynamic, unceasing plan of Creation. As the baby comes forth, either abdominally or *per vias naturales*, from its intrauterine home into the extrauterine world, there is always a reaction of either great joy or great sadness (in the event of stillbirth or an abnormality). But the admirable thing about women, even teenagers, is their courage and stamina.

If one dare offer advice to modern women, it is this. Don't have a home birth for your first delivery. The course of labor is quite unpredictable. Once you get over a first birth, there are fewer complications in subsequent ones. For a first baby choose an experienced obstetrician, that is, one who is well trained and doing at least 100 personal deliveries a year. (For many years I was doing over 300 a year.) Don't go to an obstetrician who also acts as an abortionist; you will not have the confidence that he really cares about the interests of your baby during pregnancy or labor.

If you are over 30, don't opt for a home birth. Take advantage of the safety aspects of hospital care, and then go home the next day if you wish.

Some of the hysteria surrounding childbearing has been caused by the medical profession itself, especially when the question of age is considered. It is obvious that Nature has made women fertile from age

15 to 45, give or take 2 - 3 years. In other words, that is the design of the Creator. But the medical profession knows better. It has decreed that the age range should be limited to 20 - 35 because of the problems encountered in younger or older mothers. I have always held that these problems have been exaggerated and have adhered to the physiological principle that, if a patient of whatever age is able to conceive, she is also able to deliver.

The age range of my patients was 12 - 48; in the teenagers there was never any unusual cause for alarm. In the older mothers the current hysteria relates to fetal abnormality, principally Down's syndrome (Mongolism), but even in the oldest group the risk is still small, certainly less than that of the antenatal techniques used to diagnose it.

I therefore ask the question of students or residents: What would you say if I asked you to have a laboratory test, say, a blood test, but the test would be of no benefit to you, it would be for some other person, say, your employer? And there would be a 1 - 5 percent chance that the test would either kill you or cause you serious injury?

The usual reply is rejection out of hand. But this is exactly what we are asking of the fetus when an amniocentesis (a needle sampling of the baby's liquor) or chorionic villus sampling (CVS) is performed (taking some of the placental material through the cervix or by a needle through the abdomen).

This clever technique, performed under ultrasonic scan control, can now diagnose a wide range of congenital abnormalities or diseases, the main ones apart from Down's syndrome being neural tube defects (anencephaly, or spina bifida), thalassaemia, Huntington's chorea, etc. Amniocentesis is usually performed soon after 16 weeks, when there is sufficient liquor, but it takes a further two weeks before the laboratory report is received. CVS can be done before 10 weeks and the laboratory can report in a couple of days.

A distinction must be made between early amniocentesis (at 16 - 20 weeks) and late amniocentesis (about 30 weeks). The latter procedure is commonly used to diagnose the extent to which an Rh sensitized child is affected and to plan out its treatment on this assessment. It is therefore therapeutic in intent, it is for the benefit of the baby, and, of course, quite licit.

With early amniocentesis or CVS the scenario is quite different. The whole thrust of the investigation is to decide whether or not to abort the baby, but it is obvious that most of the patients do not realize that when they embark on this exciting new procedure. They focus only on the happy day when the smiling doctor says to the smiling patient, "Your baby is all right!" And he may even be able to tell her, "It's a boy!" The smile tends to fade when she finds herself landed with a huge fee for this information which she realizes in the cold light of day is actually of no benefit to her or the baby.

It cannot be stressed too much, in fact it should be written down for the patient to read in advance, that: *There is no point in having an amniocentesis unless there is a prior decision to have an abortion in the event of an unfavorable report.* If the mother is not one who goes in for abortion, it is an illogical and unnecessary risk to undertake these investigations.

What risks? For the mother there is very little risk — although I myself would be very nervous if a doctor were to start pushing a huge long needle into my abdomen! The main risks are to the baby, and even though the statistical dangers might be slight it is naive to assume that one could interfere with an early pregnancy without some hazards, either to the baby or to the pregnancy itself.

The incidence of significant fetal abnormality is about one percent. It would be quite foolish to expose the baby to a mortality risk greater than this merely to make the diagnosis. Hanson[1] reported a fetal loss rate of 4.7 percent among amniocentesis cases handled by experts. These were nearly all normal babies. Hagge[2] in 1000 CVS cases had an accidental abortion rate of 5.4 percent. Fiddes[3] stated from a study of the world literature that the loss rate after CVS ranged from 1.2 to 14.6 percent; and in a large United States series of 2278 cases the normal babies lost were between 2.3 and 5.6 percent. These disastrous results are tolerated by obstetricians in their zeal to eliminate the abnormal.

1. Hanson, F.W. *et al.* "Amniocentesis before 15 weeks gestation." *Amer. J. Obstet. Gynec.* (1987). *156*, 1524-31.
2. Hagge, W.A. *et al.* "CVS: experience of the first 1000 cases." *Amer. J. Obstet. Gynec.* (1986). *154*, 1249-52.
3. Fiddes, T.M. *et al.* "Early prenatal diagnosis of genetic abnormality by CVS." *NZ Med. J.* (1990). *103*, 157-8.

The majority of the fetal deaths are therefore in "innocent bystanders." But who would have the nerve to condemn CVS? The unfortunate patients do not know what they are consenting to.

But that is not the end of the story. If abortion does not occur, there are still many ill-effects which do not show up until later in the pregnancy. The report of the Medical Research Council[4] covering nine major hospitals in Britain lists the following: premature rupture of the membranes and premature delivery; unexplained respiratory distress in the baby at birth; orthopaedic problems, mainly talipes (club foot) and congenital dislocation of the hips; increased incidence of Caesarean deliveries, of perinatal mortality and morbidity, of Rh sensitization, and of antepartum hemorrhage (placenta praevia or abruption).

Besides these, there have been reports in the journals of needle stick injuries in the fetus or cord — cord bleeding; loss of an eye from a needle prick; failure to develop in an arm that was pricked; a bizarre abdominal wall hernia; and so on.

The patient who refuses to have one of these ingenious diagnostic procedures is therefore protecting herself and her baby from many hazards that she had not foreseen. Maybe Holy Mother Church, opposing antenatal genetic screening and selective abortion, is so silly after all.

Case Report

My saddest case in this area was a woman who married late and had her first baby without any trouble when she was 35. At 37 she was pregnant again, but by this time the exciting new advance of amniocentesis was all the rage with doctors who had sufficient intelligence but only confused ethical standards. She was seen at the antenatal clinic by two professors. (This is mentioned to stress that she was not being handled by plain ordinary doctors.) They advised her to have this procedure. "We recommend it to everyone over the age

---

4. M.R.C. Working Party. "An assessment of the hazards of amniocentesis." *Brit. J. Obstet. Gynaec.* (1978). *85*, Supplement No. 2, p. 1-41.

of 37. It will tell us if your baby is all right." "How nice," she thought. But the tap was unsuccessful, so she was asked to come back the next week.

At the next visit she was seen by another professor and by a clever young doctor who later became a professor. They obtained some liquor (which later showed that the baby was quite normal) but the baby died the next day. Then she had to undergo further brilliant procedures to get the dead fetus delivered.

When I saw her, she was aged 40 and had been unable to conceive again. In fact it was unlikely that she would have another baby. A domestic tragedy, but in the medical statistics she would feature only as a miscarriage. She had no idea of what she was letting herself in for. She was left only with bitter tears for the child she had lost.

CHAPTER 3

Contraception

CONTRACEPTION is the success story of the century. In the 19th century it was advocated mainly by the militant atheists, Charles Bradlaugh and Annie Besant. (Besant later became a leader of the Theosophists, an early "New Age" group.) Early in the 20th century the banner was carried on by Margaret Sanger in the United States and Marie Stopes in England. Their philosophy has been embraced by the great majority of the Churches and of the population at large. Almost alone the Roman Catholic Church has stood out against this stampede down the Gadarene slope and her courageous and clear-sighted stance provides one more support to her claim to be "the one true church," the authority in matters of faith and morals.

There is no doubt that most of the advocates for contraception are actuated by the noble motive of wanting to relieve suffering women from the burdens of childbearing, but the key question is: by what method? There are licit ways and others which are illicit. Of course, the idea of having sex but avoiding having babies is such a basic and appealing one that it is not surprising to find that it has cropped up throughout recorded history.

Professor J.T. Noonan published the definitive study, *Contraception*, in 1966 (Cambridge, MA: Harvard University Press) and nothing has been written in the intervening years to equal it for scholarship and history. The main Old Testament reference to this subject is the story of Onan, who had to marry his dead brother's widow.

"Then Judah said to Onan, 'Go to your brother's wife, perform your duty as brother-in-law, and raise up seed for your brother.' Onan knew

- *45* -

that the descendants would not be his own, so whenever he had relations with his brother's wife, he let (the seed) be lost on the ground, in order not to raise up seed for his brother. What he did displeased Yahweh, who killed him also." (Genesis 38:8-10)

It has always been accepted that Onan's sin was that of *coitus interruptus,* that is, withdrawal, which is the oldest and simplest form of birth control. Onanism has always been the theologian's generic term for contraception. But there are many exegetes who now claim that Onan's fault was his failure to comply with the levirate law of inheritance.

To the simple layman, such devious exegesis takes on the air of untrustworthy special pleading. If there is any reasonable doubt about interpretation of Scripture, the judgment of the magisterium is decisive. In the case quoted above it appears to support the traditional analysis of the story.

All that has changed over the years is man's inventiveness in producing new techniques of avoiding pregnancy. Besides *coitus interruptus,* the condom has been the time-honored method of contraception. The next great development in contraceptive technology came in the mid-20th century.

"THE PILL" AND AFTER

The introduction of oral contraception (OC, or the pill) in 1960 was of greater significance for society than the atomic bomb. "The sexual revolution" (unrestrained sex and no children) had firmly arrived and its destructive effects will be felt for the next hundred years. While the original aim of the scientists might have been to help women, the power that it placed in doctors' hands introduced other concepts which were somewhat less disinterested. When in 1980 a symposium was arranged to celebrate 20 years of OC, the speakers revealed that they chose Puerto Rico for their original clinical trials in order to cut down the growth rate of these new American citizens. Since then many other countries have used the pill for population control or genocidal purposes, notably in Singapore and China.

Soon after this the intrauterine device (IUD) was introduced, a biologically inert form, usually in plastic, which remained in the womb for indefinite durations. Its great selling point was that it required no input from the woman. It therefore seemed suitable for Third World people, who in that patronizing medical way were assumed to be illiterate or stupid. No surprisingly the IUD was found to be dangerous, sometimes causing death, and A.H. Robins Ltd., manufacturer of the once popular Dalkon shield, has been forced into bankruptcy by damage claims.

The other great success story, besides contraception itself, has been the rise of the Family Planning Association (FPA), the Planned Parenthood Federation of America (PPFA) and the International Planned Parenthood Federation (IPPF) in London. These organizations have budgets in the billion dollar range, they are supported by huge private foundations and they receive millions of taxpayers' funds but they still react defensively to criticism in a way that reveals a basic insecurity. They tremble when the Catholic mouse roars. Yet they have achieved about a 75 percent penetration of the population in most Western countries and their subversion of the Catholic groups had been almost equally successful.

It is sometimes hard to remind oneself that the worldwide acceptance of contraception is such a recent sociological phenomenon. Prior to 1930 almost all the Christian Churches were officially opposed to it, even if their members were privately being converted to the new sexual freedom. The critical event which changed all this was the Anglican Lambeth Conference in June, 1930, at which the bishops for the first time approved of contraception if it was undertaken prayerfully and thoughtfully and for some serious reason.

The FPA and their allies were quick to realize that this was their great breakthrough into respectability and social acceptance.

But there were a few, besides the Catholic Church, who could see disaster ahead. One of the remarkable statements was that of Anglican Bishop Charles Gore, who said that if contraception were accepted it would eventually lead on to sodomy. This created an uproar. But what his critics could not envisage was that contraception leads on inexorably to sterilization, then to abortion and finally to homosexuality.

An unlikely critic of the new sexual philosophy was George Bernard Shaw, who stated that contraception (then only by condom) was nothing more than mutual masturbation, that is, each partner achieving the climax with no relationship to fertility. Who would have imagined that G.B.S. would ever be an ally of the papists?

Gore's prescience must be seen as remarkable. His assessment of the sexual situation was quite accurate and his prediction has come to pass. Homosexuality is already here and it has been welcomed by all the contraceptive organizations. Or, *per contra*, it has not been opposed by their Churches.

CATHOLIC TEACHING

In December, 1930, Pope Pius XI issued the first of a series of great encyclicals and papal statements on the issues of Christian marriage, contraception, sterilization and abortion.

In *Casti Connubii* (Of Christian Marriage) the Pope enunciated the traditional and unchangeable teaching of sexual morality:

"The Catholic Church, to whom God has himself committed the integrity and decency of morals, now standing in this ruin of morals, raises her voice aloud through our mouth, in sign of her divine mission, in order to keep the chastity of the nuptial bond free from this evil error, and again promulgates:

"Any use whatever of marriage, in the exercise of which the act by human effort is deprived of its natural power of procreating life, violates the law of God and of nature, and those who do such a thing are stained with a grave and mortal sin."

This is the Vicar of Christ teaching with clear and awesome authority. Who would dare to challenge him?

A commonly expressed dissident opinion among lay people and some theologians is that the new society with new circumstances and new brilliant contraceptive techniques will demand a revision of these principles which might have been adequate for the simple life of the past, but which are now quite irrelevant in the modern world.

Pope Pius XII pointed out the fallacy of that line of reasoning in his Address to Italian Midwives (1951):

"The precept is in force today, as it was yesterday, and will be so tomorrow and always, because it is not a simple injunction of human law but is the expression of both natural law and divine law."

Pope John XXIII did not make any official pronouncement on the common sexual issues, but in response to many questions he set up an international commission during the Second Vatican Council (1962-65) to enquire into them. This produced a famous (or notorious) "majority report" which favored relaxation of the prohibition of contraception, and a "minority report" supporting the constant Catholic teaching. These were leaked to the Press and many people assumed that a fateful change in the historic teaching was imminent. Forgetting that the commission had only an advisory role and that the Church is not a democracy (that is, she is not bound by simple majority opinions) they decided to "jump the gun" and opt for contraception.

I have a passing acquaintance with three members of the majority group, and I must say that I was profoundly unimpressed with their intellectual quality and their judgment.

To show how these so-called intellectuals are capable of making statements that are incomprehensible or illogical or just plain silly, the following are quotes from their *Documentum Syntheticum de Moralitate Regulationis Navitatum* (Combined Report on the Morality of Birth Control). Contraception was defined as "fostering love responsibly towards generous fecundity" (which really means: irresponsibly hoping for love through a mean sterility). Sterilization was "a marriage-stabilizing act" (often it is the first step towards marriage breakdown). And abortion for psychiatric indications was "a life and death preserving act" (presumably this really means life-preserving, but abortion more often than not makes the psychiatric state worse; and moreover the operation for this reason is commonly recognized as a clinical fraud).

Pope Paul VI was an unconscionable time in issuing his famous encyclical, *Humanae Vitae* (HV). The Pope was suspected of dithering and timidity, but when his equally courageous teaching was finally promulgated in 1968 it was met with both praise and condemnation, the reason being that it simply reiterated the unchanging principles that artificial contraception is wrong in essence and therefore harmful in its application. Great numbers of faithful Catholics were relieved to realize that their faith in the magisterium had been confirmed.

And it was not only Catholics who realized the great significance of this encyclical. Dr. Siegfried Ernst, of Ulm, Germany, one of the leading pro-life doctors in Europe, wrote:

"There is no better test for the office of Peter than that its occupant proves to be a *petros*, a rock on which all Christians can depend, so that the church will not be overcome by the gates of Hell. Contrary to Dr. [Hans] Kung and his friends, many Lutherans, among them many doctors, thank Pope Paul for *Humanae Vitae*. Indeed many were relieved. They had feared that the last moral bulwark and spiritual authority remaining in the modern world which had not yet capitulated to the golden calf might fall down on its knees before Baal and worship the spirit of the sexual revolution. Considering the unusual pressure to do so, both from within and outside the church, these fears were highly warranted."[1]

In *Humanae Vitae*, the Pope made several introductory observations and then in n. 11 he came to the heart of the matter in this solemn declaration:

"Nonetheless the church, calling men back to the observance of the norms of the natural law, as interpreted by her constant doctrine, teaches that each and every marriage act must remain open to the transmission of life."

In other words, only normal intercourse is permissible; if the act is embarked upon it must be carried through normally; and nothing may be done to wreck the fertile nature of intercourse. In this one brilliant sentence the Pope provided a formula which covered untercourse in every circumstance of life, even if fertility is absent (say, after the menopause, or after hysterectomy, or in conditions of sterility, whether temporary or permanent). Even if pregnancy is impossible, the couple are bound to normal intercourse; their marriage does not give them rights to all forms of perverted sexual actions.

When the encyclical was promulgated in July, 1968, Fr. Charles Curran, Professor of Theology at Catholic University of America, Washington, D.C., organized an immediate protest against it. He had probably been forewarned but, with remarkable efficiency, he had full

---

1. Ernst, S. *Man the Greatest of Miracles.* The Liturgical Press, Collegeville, MN (1976), p. 132.

page advertisements in the main American dailies within 24 hours protesting against the teaching and advising people to follow their own consciences. About 70 Catholic theologians signed this public statement of defiance of the Pope. Curran was able to boast:

"Our quick, forceful response supported by so many theologians accomplished its purpose. Catholics could read in their morning papers about their right to dissent and the fact that Catholics could in theory and in practice disagree with papal teaching and still be loyal Roman Catholics."[2]

This was, of course, what the Americans call "hogwash." People soon realized that one cannot insult the Pope publicly, reject magisterial teaching and still be a loyal Catholic. Anyone who does is *ipso facto* a disloyal Catholic, and he might as well face up to the truth. Modern society is bamboozled by innumerable examples of what George Orwell called "newspeak" in which words mean exactly the opposite of what they say. Curran was an exponent of this technique.

The bishops and university authorities were paralyzed by intellectual timidity, pride and the false claims of academic freedom. It took Curran just 24 hours to sabotage the Pope; it took the church leaders 20 years before they had the nerve to dismiss Curran from his teaching post.

To their credit, many of the original signers later withdrew their support for Curran when they realized how wrong he was and how it is impossible to oppose the Pope in matters of faith or morals. With admirable humility Professor William May explained some years later how he, probably like so many other younger theologians, thought to himself that Curran and his supporters were the *literati* at that time and who would have the courage to oppose them? Anyone with the childlike faith of Louis Pasteur's paradigmatic "Breton peasant" would have had the insight and the courage to support the Holy Father.

Curran was not the only antipapal voice. Many bishops, imagining intolerable burdens being imposed upon married couples, forgot their vows of loyalty to the Vicar of Christ and rejected his teaching. Two of them in the United States abandoned their sees and got married, one of these romantic unions being to a divorcée in the Church of Christ. The

---

2. Muggeridge, Ann Roche. *The Desolate City.* Harper and Row, San Francisco, 1986.

root cause of these tragedies was obviously something more than a simple issue of contraception. Fourteen national Bishops' Conferences failed to support the encyclical and advised their people to follow their own consciences like sheep without a shepherd.

The most notable among the English-speaking countries was the Canadian hierarchy who, at their meeting in Winnipeg in September, 1968, stated that: "persons who have tried sincerely but without success to pursue a line of conduct in keeping with the given directives may be safely assured that whoever choose that course which seems right to them do so in good conscience."

While the sentence construction might seem ponderous and obscure, the faithful soon realized that it really meant: "in the matter of contraception, please yourselves," which they did on a grand scale. Twenty years later the Canadian birth rate and family size were alarmingly low (especially in Quebec, the most Catholic province), and abortion, the inevitable sequel to contraception, was flourishing everywhere.

But there is one ray of hope. In 1989 the Bishops of Manitoba stated: ". . . in the past 20 years many Catholic couples appear to have simply made up their own minds to disregard *Humanae Vitae*." And they went on to point out that the often quoted escape clause, conscience, "ought to be conformed to the law of God in the light of the teaching authority of the Church, which is the authentic interpreter of divine law." Better late than never.

There is no doubt that the contraceptive issue is for most ordinary people the main moral problem, and therefore the main reason that so many abandon religious practice. Either they do not understand the real nature of contraception, or they feel that the Catholic way of life is too onerous. This is a tragedy. On the one hand contraceptive living often leads to personal and national disaster while on the other, as millions have realized, God's plan in marriage as outlined by the Church is the only one which will bring happiness and grace. As Our Lord said, His burden is light and His yoke is sweet. Do we really believe this? It is the modern test of faith.

WHAT'S WRONG WITH CONTRACEPTION?

This is the key question. If artificial contraception is wrong in essence we may not use it, even if it were to make us all healthy and wealthy. The ethical assessment of any human action depends on three factors: the act itself (this is the objective judgment), the intention (the subjective judgment), and the circumstances.

Considering this last factor, if there were, say, duress or ignorance or State intervention in the contraception decision, the moral fault might be diminished or even absent.

Assessing a person's intentions is quite impossible for any second party. Only God can read the human heart. But it would be fairly safe to assume that for most people using contraception their ignorance, or fear, or social pressure would probably reduce their level of culpability to minimal, or even nil.

On the other hand, for Catholics this excuse might not be acceptable. The least educated section of the laity might be able to say in defence, "We didn't know any better. We never had any guidance in homilies or episcopal statements." But those theologians and educators who advocate contraception will eventually have to answer the question: "Why did you not listen to the teachings of my Popes?" It will be a difficult problem for them to cope with before the Throne of Grace.

This leads us to the most important consideration, the act itself. The nature of contraception can be assessed by considering first the generic or overall concept of this act; and then each individual type of contraceptive must be examined to see how it conforms to the three main virtues in marriage — love, justice and purity.

The essence of contraception is that it divorces the sex act from its fertile nature. Note that the phrase is not: "from pregnancy." With any single act of intercourse, pregnancy is unlikely to occur; and in some sterile circumstances it is quite impossible.

Nevertheless, on the one hand marriage rights extend only to normal intercourse, whether fertile or not; and on the other we may not separate the love-giving and the life-giving elements of sex. It is obvious from the design of the Creator, the anatomy and physiology of the reproductive organs, that these two elements, love and life, are inseparable. The donation of both from each spouse to the other must be simultaneous because they are inherent in the nature of the act.

This is not simply a cold analytical approach. Its importance can be seen in the *in vitro* fertilization (IVF) analogy. Contraception offers sex without babies. IVF means babies without sex. Each may be undertaken in love but each is wrong for the same reason, the separation of intercourse from fertility. This provides an interesting anomaly — one act aims to abolish fertility, the other to enhance it.

All contraceptives act either through altering the essential nature of intercourse or by deranging the reproductive system in various ways, such as by suppressing ovulation, killing off the sperm, destroying the function of cervix, uterus or tubes, and so on. Marriage rights do not permit us to do these things. It is often assumed that marriage is *carte blanche* for any form of sexual activity, but this is not so. These rights are limited only to normal vaginal sex and the preliminaries leading up to it.

METHODS OF CONTRACEPTION

A brief assessment can now be made as to how the common contraceptives work:

1. *Coitus interruptus* — "withdrawal," "being careful," etc. Interruption of the act before ejaculation, the oldest and simplest method of avoiding pregnancy, the historic sin of Onan. This is an offence against purity.

2. *Barrier methods* — condom, diaphragm, cervical cap and a few other obnoxious variations on the same theme. These act by preventing access of sperms to ovum. They alter the essential nature of the male and female organs, the penis becoming a simple phallus and the vagina an indifferent cavity. Intercourse in these circumstances becomes essentially, as George Bernard Shaw said, mutual masturbation, and therefore an impure act. It is similar to the use of artificial sex organs from the local sex shop.

3. *Hormonal methods* — mainly oral contraception ("the pill"), or Depo-Provera (a three-monthly intramuscular injection), or Norplant subdermal implants which are left in place for five years on end. These hormones have multiple effects on the reproductive system, but the main one appears to be a medical sterilization through suppression of ovulation. Despite the millions of women using them, the exact mode of action is still uncertain. They alter the nature and viscosity of mucus in the cervix, and this prevents penetration by the sperm cells. As they do not suppress ovulation in every cycle or in every woman yet still achieve remarkable efficacy, it is assumed that they must sometimes act as abortifacients. That is, fertilization occurs but the new pregnancy fails to implant, possibly because there is atrophy of the endometrium.

Whether as sterilizers or abortifacients, they involve an offence against justice (the Fifth Commandment).

4. *Intrauterine device* (IUD) — plastic forms, sometimes copper-coated or hormone-impregnated, which remain within the womb permanently. They almost certainly act as abortifacients, preventing the implantation of the fertilized ovum. This is also an offence against justice. And it exposes the illogical stance of those who say, "I am in favor of contraception, but I wouldn't have anything to do with abortion." IUD users are already involved in abortion, but without knowing it.

5. *Vaginal creams, jellies or pessaries* — these spermicidal agents are inserted before intercourse and hope to kill off the sperms, often with indifferent success. They are essentially medical and temporary sterilizing agents, and on those grounds they are unacceptable.

6. *"The morning after pill"* — this is a massive dose of estrogen hormone taken in the cold light of day when the woman begins to have second thoughts about the events of the night before. It is also used in cases of alleged rape. Its mode of action remains unclear but it mainly aims to so alter the endometrium that, if fertilization does occur, the pregnancy will not implant. This is an abortifacient action. It has a 1-2 percent failure rate, and if pregnancy should occur there is an increased risk of its being ectopic (in the tube) which in some cases can be fatal.

7. *"Menstrual extraction"* — groups of feminists often use this on one another, either to shorten the duration of the menstrual flow or to

abort an early pregnancy if conception should have occurred. A fine tube, attached to a large syringe, is inserted through the cervix into the uterus and the contents are sucked out. As it is performed only a few days after intercourse, most of the women are uncertain if they are actually pregnant. If they should be, the device is obviously an abortifacient.

8. *Physiological methods* — "natural family planning" (NFP) based on ovulation detection and restricting intercourse to the infertile parts of the menstrual cycle. As this preserves normal sexual activity and offends against neither purity nor justice, it involves no moral fault.

SELECTION OF METHOD OF CONTRACEPTION

Married (and not infrequently, unmarried) couples often ask each other, and doctors ask patients, "What method of family planning to use?" The question seems superfluous for anyone with moral insight. It is obvious that all the artificial methods are wrong in principle and also in their detailed application, but this fact is not clearly appreciated by the majority of the population. While this deficiency is excusable in those who have no religious or philosophical education, it is difficult to understand in priests, religious and lay Catholics, all of whom have the additional advantage of magisterial guidance. The logical deduction is that there is actually no "choice" of methods. It is a matter of NFP or nothing.

The common fallacy is the assumption that it is impossible to achieve happiness and sexual bliss without that little pill (or IUD, etc.).

If theologians and others are not convinced by the simple ethical argument against contraception, at least they should be persuaded by the pragmatic consideration of the often unforeseen consequences of its acceptance by individuals and by society. The Popes, guided by the Holy Spirit, could see these disasters clearly and everything predicted by Paul VI in *Humanae Vitae* has come to pass. But still, over 20 years later, prominent theologians such as Frs. Charles Curran, Hans Kung, and Bernard Haering are making pleas to give Catholics access to contraception. Do they realize what they are asking for? The following list reveals the harm done by this crazy logic.

UNEXPECTED SEQUELAE OF CONTRACEPTION

1. It is the first step to acceptance of the antinatalism that is destroying Western countries. Individuals, as well as societies, must opt for either pronatalism (in favor of births) or antinatalism (rejection of childbearing).

2. It is the first step in the antinatalist triad. There is an *inevitable progression* from contraception to sterilization and then to abortion. Once contraception is introduced, it is only a matter of time before sterilization and abortion arrive. Or, arguing retrospectively, if a community accepts abortion it must necessarily have accepted the other two elements of the triad.

Put in another way, if the Abortion Law Reform Association (ALRA) or one of the abortion chains in the United States, where they are franchised like Kentucky Fried Chicken, wanted to introduce this practice into an unsophisticated country (say, of the Pacific Islands), it would be impossible because of their religious nature. But, if they once got the Island people started on contraception it would not take long before abortion became acceptable.

It is therefore misleading for the FPA to advocate more contraception as a prophylaxis against abortion, "because then only wanted babies would be conceived." This is an attractive theory, but the facts prove the opposite. The graphs of contraceptive dissemination and abortion incidence are *not* reciprocally varying; instead, they both rise in parallel. Why should this be? Because at base both are expressions of antinatalism. This is further confirmed by the observation that in every country the personnel of the FPA and the ALRA (or their equivalents) are virtually identical or interchangeable.

The fateful progression from contraception to abortion can be seen in the recent history of society and of the medical profession. Fifty years ago contraception was being introduced, but any doctor procuring abortion was prosecuted. Now the profession is saturated with both activities, and the non-aborting doctor suffers from professional ostracism.

Further painful experience of life has shown in recent years that this "progression" should really be expected at both ends. Before contraception insert masturbation; after abortion add homosexuality. Once again, the accuracy of this observation is incontrovertible. This is exactly what has happened in society and in individual lives. And the common factor in all these activities is: antinatalism.

Many people are not prepared to believe this. The idea is preposterous, they say. How can taking a little pill in a responsible way lead on to disgusting homosexuality? Perhaps they will believe a clergyman who is also a homosexual. Leighton Johnson[3] quotes Rev. Richard Kirker, the General Secretary of the Gay Christian Movement in Britain, in a dramatic article that reveals the alarming spread of homosexuality among clergy and religious of all denominations.

Kirker "held that the roles of ordained minister and practicing homosexual were quite consistent since this logically flowed from the Anglican Church's radical alteration of its teaching as to the purposes of the sexual act through its changed teaching on contraception at the 1930 Lambeth Conference.

"Rev. Kirker pointed out that when his Church thus supported contraception it had nullified the proposition that procreation had to be the sole, or main, purpose of sexual relations. The main purpose could then be defined as simply sexual pleasure. So, 'if sex can be valid for the pleasure it gives heterosexuals,' he stated, 'gay people can enjoy their form of sex in the same way.' "

3. Contraception facilitates, and therefore encourages, all premarital and extramarital liaisons, making society into a sexual jungle, as every distressed wife or mother will agree.

---

3. Johnson, L. "Homosexuality." *AD 2000*, July, 1990, p. 9.

Case Report

O n e of my patients, aged about 45, a simple but good woman with no definite religious affiliation, an admirable wife and mother, once said to me: "That b. . . pill! It's lost me, my husband, my marriage, my home, my daughter and the baby I should have had years ago."

The story was that she had two children and wanted to have another, but her husband said they could not afford it. She disagreed but she started on the pill and kept taking it for some years. It made her fat and irritable and turned her off sex. Like many ageing husbands this one tried his hand at extramarital sex with a younger woman who, of course, was also on the pill. Meanwhile the teenage daughter, also taking the pill, became sexually involved with an older man and left home to live with him in a de facto union. The female interloper, probably more by design than by accident, then became pregnant. This led to a divorce and the husbands remarriage, while his new wife had the baby which my friend would dearly love to have had. It was a multiple tragedy, but it is being repeated a thousand times every day.

E ach of the three women went to the same family planning clinic, and it is very likely that the FPA doctor who provided them with their pills would have praised them for being so "responsible" about sex. This is the standard party line.

4. Since the beginning of the world sex has been regarded, human frailty excepted, as the privilege of the married state. This has obviously been the design of the Creator, but with the advent of contraception every Tom, Dick and Harry, married or unmarried, goes in for sterile sex. The married state has therefore been depreciated, even denigrated, as something unnecessary in society. Freed from the burdens of childbearing, permanency and fidelity, marriage has become undervalued and derogated, and *de facto* unions abound.

5. The rejection of childbearing has contributed to the estrangement of teenagers from their parents in what is called "the generation gap." The children soon come to know if their parents have embraced the antinatalist triad. If so, they realize that the parents do not really like

children; in fact, with the prevalence of abortion, they are lucky to be alive. They have been robbed of the brothers and sisters whom they should have had, and their upbringing has been warped. They see the materialism and hedonism of their parents who prefer sterile sex and money to children.

6. Contraception in Catholic marriages leads to neglect of the sacraments and the spiritual life, considerations which are quite beyond the comprehension of your average FPA doctor.

7. Contraception has been a major factor in the demographic collapse of Western countries, and all those who recommend it or prescribe it must bear some of the responsibility for the phenomenon of ageing populations. This also has repercussions on the inherent vitality of a country's social life. Without the stimulus of young people's ideas and optimism, a city seems to be running down. Behind the contraceptive program there is a hidden rationale of misanthropy and xenophobia. At heart the family planners really do hate people, and also foreigners, especially if they are of a different color. This came out in the writings of Margaret Sanger, who had a profound antipathy towards the poor and the blacks. She was enamored of the idea of eugenics achieved through the familiar antinatalist techniques.

This is now having an impact on the economy, and that will hurt all of us in our pockets. Too late society has realized that people are not a curse, they are a blessing; an asset, not a liability; they are not just "mouths to feed," they are hands to work with, consumers to provide demand, brains to think with, hearts to love with.

8. A surprising consequence of contraception, both within the Catholic group and in the wider society, is that it makes a significant contribution to the current shortage of vocations to the priesthood and the religious life. One obvious explanation is the reduction in the number of children. Just a few years ago the average family size among Catholics was about four children, the range being approximately 0 - 10. St. Ignatius Loyola (d. 1556), founder of the Jesuits, was the last of 13 children. If his parents had lived in the modern world, he might never have been born. Now Catholics are hardly distinguishable from their unchurched friends with their two children per family.

But another deleterious repercussion of contraception on vocations is less obvious because it is more subtle. In all previous ages the Evangelical Counsels were an essential feature of religious life — poverty, chastity and obedience. Poverty and obedience have been watered down somewhat, but chastity remains unchanged.

The renunciation of the noble state of marriage, of married love and of childbearing was always seen as the courageous sacrifice which the young person made for the sake of Christ and His apostolate. But now that marriage has been devalued, that a permanent lifelong contract is rejected, and that a pure fruitful love is ridiculed, the quality of the sacrifice is depreciated.

As Solomon said, "there is nothing new under the sun." (Ecclesiastes 1:9) The world has gone through similar upheavals in its long history. St. John Chrysostom (d. 407), Bishop of Constantinople, the "golden voiced" Doctor of the Church, observed that: "When marriage is not esteemed, neither can consecrated virginity or celibacy exist; when sexuality is not regarded as a great value given by the Creator, the renunciation of it for the sake of the Kingdom of Heaven loses its meaning."

This, then, is what the permissives are asking for when they plead for papal permission to take a little pill (or other contraceptive). Their lack of vision is astounding. To give only one example, take *The Tablet* (London), which has adopted a consistently anti-papal stance in recent years, notably under its previous editor, Tom Burns. Writing on the occasion of the paper's 150th anniversary, Burns[4] described his excitement on receiving the "majority report" before *Humanae Vitae* was promulgated:

"I rushed the full report into print in three successive issues and the reverberations were immense." When it was eventually proclaimed, Burns wrote: "The encyclical . . . ignored the years of specialized discussion and the decisions of the Pope's own commission . . . resting itself mainly on much earlier papal statements." In this Burns was quite wrong. The Pope did quote previous encyclicals, but his main reason for rejecting contraception was that it is forbidden in principle by both

---

4. *The Tablet*, 19 May, 1980.

natural law and revealed divine law. Burns went on to say: "I took counsel with myself and with a leading Jesuit . . . Fr. Corbishley, and with Fr. Arthur McCormack, the population expert. . . ." These confirmed him in his anti-papal campaign. This was regrettable, even tragic, but it was typical of much of the "intellectual" opposition which the Pope suffered in those days.

Subsequent Popes have been saddened to see Paul VI's predictions come true, notably the ill-effects on women and on marriage.

HEALTH HAZARDS

This leads on naturally to a consideration of any risks to health in the use of various contraceptives. Most women ask themselves this question sooner or later, but in fact it is a matter of only secondary importance. Even if contraceptives were the elixir of life and capable of bringing health to everyone, their use would still be wrong on moral grounds.

A brief consideration of the health risks of the common contraceptives will be of interest, not least because, for obvious reasons, this sort of information is not often publicized.

We have always believed that *barrier methods* did not pose any health hazards, apart from local vaginal sensitivity reactions to rubber and spermicidal chemicals, but a completely new outlook on the matter has come from a most interesting recent article. In a unique investigation[5] researchers from the North Carolina Memorial Hospital tested their hypothesis "that contraceptive methods that prevent exposure to sperm and seminal fluid (condoms, diaphragms, spermicides, withdrawal) are associated with a higher risk of preeclampsia."

They investigated 110 patients having their first babies and matched them with a similar group who differed only in not having used barrier methods. The barrier group had a preeclampsia risk that was 2.37 times that of the control group. Admittedly the numbers are small, but the

5. Klonoff-Cohen, H.S. *et al.* "An Epidemiologic Study of Contraception and Preeclampsia." *J. American Med. Ass.* (1989), *262*, 3143-47.

results are persuasive. The Editorial in the same issue (p. 3184) agreed with "this exciting thesis." It pointed out that preeclampsia is "a leading cause of maternal morbidity and mortality, intrauterine growth retardation, and perinatal morbidity and mortality (that is, stillbirths plus neonatal deaths)."

Preeclampsia (or, toxemia of pregnancy, as it used to be called) is a mystery disease whose cause has never been discovered in spite of over 50 years of intensive study. It affects mainly first pregnancies but what has emerged in recent "sex revolution" years is that the emphassis should perhaps be concentrated on the male. This is because the risk returns when mothers who have had children conceive again with a new husband, or a new partner, or if they receive the semen of a stranger in artificial insemination by donor (A.I.D.).

It seems that the female body should normally absorb sperms or seminal fluid through the reproductive tract for some gradual mysterious change to occur in the immune system which will protect her from toxemia. It has been known for some time that in laboratory animals injections of semen will encourage full development of the female uterus and related organs. Something similar may be necessary for the wellbeing of the human female. Once again the ingenuity of the Creator's design is revealed, and the lesson is learned that only physiological intercourse should be permitted.

The greatest concern is caused by *hormone contraception* (OC) because these are steroid chemicals and therefore they can affect the cells of every organ in the body. On the one hand it is a tribute to the resilience of the body and its amazing power of adaptation that it can cope with so many foreign substances ingested over the years; but on the other hand this reassurance is no consolation to the woman who has suffered a disaster.

Case Report

A mother in the next suburb to where I live found her 17-year-old daughter dead in bed. She had taken only half of her first pack of OCs. When she confronted her family doctor about the tragedy, he disclaimed any responsibility. She should have sued for a million dollars.

It is embarrassing, even grimly amusing, to recall the reassuring comments made by medical authorities in the recent past. For example, in 1962 the American Medical Association made a press statement: "There is no evidence that OC pills cause blood clotting. . . ." This was "hogwash." Final proof of the association of OCs with thrombosis and embolism came from the brilliant work of Sir Richard Doll and Dr. M.P. Vessey[6] in Oxford, and this has been confirmed many times since.

In 1967 and again in 1974 the Royal College of General Practitioners stated that there were only slight risks in taking OCs but within a few months the first report was published of a dramatic new complication, blood vessel tumors in the liver.[7] These rare tumors usually killed by causing massive intra-abdominal hemorrhage, but within a year there was "the first report of malignant transformation (cancer) of a liver tumour in a patient taking OCs."[8]

Everyone now knows that OCs are often associated with clotting problems (strokes), coronaries and high blood pressure but there is a long list of interesting minor complications which patients should be told about: skin pigmentation; gingivitis (bleeding from the gums); disturbance of phosphorus and glucose metabolism; jaundice from increased viscosity of the bile; alopecia (baldness); sterility for various reasons; depression; herpes; loss of libido (which defeats the whole aim of the exercise); chorea (involuntary movements of the limbs); visual defects (blurring of the cornea); problems with breastfeeding; and scores of others.

One of the unsolved problems which will worry mothers for many years: what will be the effect on the developing child of being dosed with estrogen and/or progesterone in breast milk at this critical age? It is idle for doctors to try to reassure patients, saying, "Ah yes, that was when we were using bigger doses, 50 micrograms of estrogen. But now we use only 30 micrograms and that is *absolutely safe.*" The only answer to that is to say: "Oh yeah?", which expresses a prudent attitude of scientific scepticism.

---

6. *British Medical Journal* (1968), *2*, 199. Also (1969), *1*, 651.
7. *British Medical Journal* (1974), *2*, 7-10. (Sullivan, J.P. and Wilding, R.P.)
8. *British Medical Journal* (1975), 29 November, 496-498.

DOES THE PILL CAUSE CANCER?

Sooner or later all women ask themselves this question. At present the answer is: we don't know. It will take many more years before a confident statement can be given, one way or the other. It is difficult to prove anything in medicine, but especially so in the cancer field. This is not much help to the woman who has to decide right now whether to embark on longtime OC intake or not, but at least she should be made aware of the available facts.

Many cancers are hormone-dependent. At present there is a fashion for HRT (hormone replacement therapy), a continuous dosage of estrogens after the menopause as a prophylaxis against future coronaries or osteoporosis (thinning of the bones leading to fracture of the hip). The risk of the medication is that it might lead to cancer of the endometrium (lining the inside of the womb), but many gynecologists claim that this risk is overcome by adding another hormone, progesterone. Activist doctors never give up. No drug, no hormone, ever strikes fear into their breasts. But as far back as 1975 two articles and two guest editorials in the same journal[9] all confirmed this cancer risk.

It is therefore not surprising that about the same time a unique cancer registry was set up by the University of Colorado, Denver: Registry for Endometrial Carcinoma (cancer) in Young Women Taking Oral Contraceptive Agents. The first 21 cases were reported soon afterwards. [10] *Res ipsa loquitur* (the matter speaks for itself).

Even though convincing proof that these hormones may cause cancer of various organs still does not exist, it will be interesting to mention just a few recent articles which highlight this possible association, leaving readers to draw their own conclusions. Where the statistical term "relative risk" occurs (that is, the increased risk for those taking the drug compared with a normal population), only the higher figure in the range will be given for the sake of simplicity. It should be remembered, of course, that if there are only a few patients in the

9. *New England Journal of Medicine* (1975), *293*, 1167-70 and 1164-67.
10. *Obstetrics and Gynecology* (1975), *46*, 503-6.

series the figures may not be "significant." The higher figure gives the "worst case scenario."

An Oxford study of 26 women with cancer of the liver (which used to be a very rare disease) showed that the use of OCs for more than eight years increased this risk x 7.2, and the risk of developing non-malignant liver tumors was increased 500-fold. ". . . (experiments) in laboratory animals . . . have shown that sex steroids (as in OCs) may act as initiators or promoters of carcinogenesis (causing cancer)."[11]

Another article in the same journal on 30 young women, aged 24-44 years, who died of liver cancer ". . . the use of OCs was associated with a significantly . . . raised relative risk . . . of 3.8, and use of OCs for 8 years or more (gave) an increased risk of 20.1"![12]

An extraordinary recent observation is the association of OCs with microadenomas (tiny non-malignant tumors) in the pituitary gland which lies on the under side of the brain and controls most of the hormone production in the body. Who wants a cerebral tumor, even if it is only microscopic in size!

Most of the reproductive organs (ovaries, endometrium, cervix, breasts) respond each month to the endogenous (formed within the body) hormones associated with the menstrual cycle. The question naturally arises: how are they affected by similar exogenous (drugs taken into the body) hormones?

The cervix, which is the easiest organ to inspect, takes on a bizarre appearance never seen in women not taking the pill. This has led to the introduction of a new diagnostic term by the pathologists: "pill cervix." Sometimes the red area surrounding the os (entrance into the canal of the cervix) becomes red and raised like a rosette, and it bleeds when touched by the spatula used in taking a cytological smear. This change is mainly a blood vessel enrichment, not a malignancy, and a similar change occurs throughout the vagina. The same changes occur in pregnancy, therefore the pill is said to induce a "pseudo-pregnancy" state.

If the gynecologist operates on the vagina (say, a vaginal repair

---

11. "OCs and hepatocellular carcinoma." Neuberger, J. *et al. British Medical J.* (1986), *292*, 1355-7.
12. Forman, D. *et al.* "Cancer of the liver and the use of OCs." *ibid.*, 1357-61.

operation), the site is flooded with blood and sometimes the operation has to be abandoned. When the pill was first introduced this bleeding effect led to many blood transfusions and the occasional death, but now gynecologists will never do pelvic operations unless the patient has discontinued the hormones for at least a month. This also reduces the risk of embolism (clotting) problems.

The link between OCs and cancer of the cervix still remains uncertain. One of the first papers to suggest a causal link was that of Dr. Martin Vessey, of Oxford. [13] In an extensive survey the following year, Cook[14] noted: "the increasing trends in both mortality and incidence." Further: "among younger women (there has been) a substantial increase in rates of cancer *in situ*. . . ." This he attributed to: "increasing exposure to a sexually transmitted agent resulting from changing patterns of sexual behavior . . . and possible direct effects of the contraceptive pill." And he pointed out that "this increase (in cancer of the cervix) was predictable." The question naturally follows: why does the Department of Health not warn the young of the dangers of promiscuity instead of following a "liberal" sexual philosophy?

One of the difficulties in establishing cause and effect in medicine arises from the fact that some diseases change their nature over the years, and this is particularly the case with cancer of the cervix. Dr. Elliott, writing from the King George V Hospital, Sydney, reviewed 2628 patients with cancer of the cervix between 1953 and 1986. He found that "the proportion of young women (aged less than 35) increased from 9 percent to about 25 percent over these 34 years." And "the disease has become more severe."[15]

Possible explanations for this change may be: promiscuity; starting sex at a young age (often about 15); having multiple male partners;

13. Vessey, M.P., *et al.* "Neoplasia (cancer) of the cervix uteri and contraception: a possible direct action of the pill." *Lancet* (1983), ii, 930.
14. Cook, C.A., *et al.* "Trends in cervical cancer and carcinoma *in situ* in Great Britain." *Brit. J. Cancer* (1984), *50*, 367-375.
15. Elliott, P.M., *et al.* "Changing character of cervical cancer in young women." *Brit. Med. J.* (1989), *298.* 288-290.

prolonged dosage with OCs from a young age; smoking (!); and becoming infected with sexually transmitted diseases, particularly the virus type. HPV (human papilloma virus) is almost certainly one cause of cancer of the cervix. The similarity to HIV (human immunovirus) which destroys the immune system response and causes AIDS is too great to ignore.

The first paper to show that OCs are associated with a higher incidence of HPV, and therefore will increase the risk of cancer of the cervix, came from Dr. Chang of the University of Otago, Dunedin. [16] He found that, in women with precancerous lesions, "those using hormone contraception had a significantly higher infection rate with HPV. . . . If hormonal contraceptive use and simultaneous HPV infection are associated with cervical neoplasia (cancer), and laboratory evidence supports this thesis, then further urgent investigations are needed, for the implications are grave." Obviously he considers that young women should be warned.

Dr. Valerie Beral[17] reported on the Royal College of General Practitioners OC Study. "Of 47,000 women followed since 1968 those who had used OCs had a significant higher incidence of cervical cancer than never-users." She found that in patients using OCs for over 10 years, the risk was increased four-fold.

Breast cancer is more common than cervix cancer, and it is appearing in younger women. Is this attributable to hormonal contraception? Once again, this proposition is difficult to prove but the evidence is very suggestive.

Two original articles and an editorial in the *Lancet* (Oct. 22, 1983) shook the medical world and made headlines in the lay press. The most impressive paper came from Prof. Pike of Los Angeles, who analyzed 314 breast cancer patients and concluded that, if they had used OCs

16. Chang, A.R. "Hormonal contraceptives, Human Papillomaviruses and cervical cancer; some observations from a colposcopy clinic." *Aust. N.Z. J. Obstet. Gynec.* (1989), *29*, 329-331.
17. Beral, V., *et al.* "Oral Contraceptive use and malignancies of the genital tract." *Lancet* (1988), *2*, 1331-5.

under the age of 25 and had taken them for more than five years, their chances of developing breast cancer were increased four-fold.[18]

McPherson[19] in a study from six London hospitals came to a similar conclusion, and stressed the suspicion that taking OCs before the first full-term pregnancy (FFTP) may be a harmful factor. The latent period between the hormone stimulus and development of cancer may be as long as 20 years.

Chilvers[20] in a large British study found that those who used OCs for more than eight years ran a 74 percent increased risk of developing breast cancer. His article stated: "the simplest and most plausible explanation must be that there is a substantial causal relation between prolonged OC use and breast cancer risk in young women."

Papers similar to this posed a major problem for the International Planned Parenthood Federation because its members prescribe OCs for millions of teenagers around the world. Their comment[21] was that the risk had been increased "to 1 in 350, still a very small one . . . there was no need to change OC prescribing practice. . . ." Of course, if they did take notice of these risks their contraceptive empire would collapse.

Another interesting study was based on the injectable hormonal contraceptive, Depo-Provera (D-P), which is a huge (150mg.) dose of progesterone given every three months. This drug is manufactured in the United States but it is considered too dangerous for patients in that country. The FDA (Food and Drug Administration) will not license it because animal experiments in beagle dogs show that it causes them to develop breast cancer.

D-P has been used in New Zealand since 1969; it is prescribed more extensively there than in any other developing country. Dr. Paul, of the University of Otago, reported the largest series of cases, 891 women

18. Pike, M.C., *et al.* "Breast cancer in young women and use of oral contraceptives." *Lancet* (1983), *2*, 926-930.
19. McPherson, K., *et al.* "Early Oral Contraceptive Use and Breast Cancer." *Brit. J. Cancer* (1987), *56*, 653-660.
20. Chilvers, C., *et al.* "Oral contraceptive use and breast cancer in young women." *Lancet* (1989), *1*, 973-982.
21. "Oral contraceptives and breast cancer." *IPPF Medical Bulletin* (1989), 4 August.

with new breast cancers, and came to the conclusion that D-P "may increase the risk of breast cancer in young women." In those aged 25-34 who had used the drug for over 6 years, the relative risk of developing cancer was (in the worst scenario) increased 21-fold. For those who were under 25 and had used it for 2 years or more, the relative risk figure was up to 15-fold. [22] If contraception were not such a sacred cow, the Department of Health should prohibit the use of D-P immediately, but health administrators as a class tend to regard themselves as "liberal," that is, afraid to oppose any aspect of the sexual revolution.

DANGERS OF INTRAUTERINE DEVICES

The three main ill effects of IUDs are: excessive bleeding, perforation of the uterus, and pelvic inflamatory disease (PID). Coincidentally, these are the three main complications of induced abortion. The IUD acts as a foreign body within the cavity of the uterus and therefore the menstrual periods tend to be prolonged and heavy. This can be a serous problem in Third World countries where malnutrition and anemia are common. The foreign body either introduces new infection or causes latent infection to flare up, causing chronic pelvic inflammation and sterility. When the IUD is poked into the uterus in a "blind" operation, it is not uncommon for it to perforate the uterine wall and come to lie free in the abdominal cavity. Sometimes the IUD is "lost" and the difficulty is to discover whether it has fallen out or gone up higher. There have been several reports of two IUDs floating about within the abdomen, a tribute to the persistence of the doctor and the trusting faith of the patient.

The worst complication, if that is the right word, is death. The cause of this tragedy, of which large numbers have been reported, is that the IUD fails, the patient becomes pregnant, she often miscarries in the second trimester and the foreign body within the uterus causes an overwhelming infection (septicemia).

22. Paul, C., *et al.* "Depo-Provera and risk of breast cancer." *Brit. Med. J.* (1989), *299*, 759-762.

Because of similar disasters the manufacturer of the original Dalkon shield, A.H. Robins Ltd., was swamped with so many claims for damage that it went bankrupt. In 1988 a jury in Minnesota awarded a woman $8.75 million damages against G.D. Searle Co., manufacturer of the popular Copper-7 IUD. A reasonable person might wonder why IUDs are not banned, but the IPPF and similar contraceptive organizations still keep using them, especially in illiterate women. Few governments or medical bodies would have the courage to confront the contraceptive moguls.

Can IUDs cause cancer? Even though it is well recognized that "chronic irritation" is one cause of cancer, not many doctors know that the answer to the question is: Yes. The cancer of the endometrium can take on a bizarre appearance, reflecting exactly the shape of the IUD. Dr. Ober[23] stated that "we now know of 12 cases in which polyethylene IUCDs seem to have either initiated or promoted the development of a uterine cancer." In primitive communities this diagnosis might never be made, even if the cancer causes death.

The dangers associated with methods of preventing pregnancy were realized by a clever young woman researcher in England a few years ago. Dr. Valerie Beral[24] wrote an historic article in which she stated: "there were more deaths at ages 25-44 in England and Wales from adverse effects of OC use than from all the complications of pregnancy, delivery and the puerperium combined." Therefore she recommended that the standard term and concept, "maternal mortality," should be replaced by "reproductive mortality."

Maternal mortality is defined differently in different countries. In general, though, it means maternal deaths during pregnancy and a variable time after delivery, sometimes 6 weeks, or 3 months, or even 12 months. The major cause of "maternal mortality" in my own country is — road accidents! In some American cities it is gunshot wounds. But most people assume it refers only to obstetric deaths. Therefore it is important to determine the facts when we hear the common statements

23. Ober, W.B. "Uterine malignancies developing after a long term use of IUCD." *Asia-Oceania J. Obstet. Gynec.* (1989), *15*, 209.
24. Beral, V. "Reproductive mortality." *Brit. Med. J.* (1979), 15 Sept., p. 632.

by the FPA or the various abortion societies, "Contraception is safer than pregnancy," or "abortion is safer. . . ." For one thing, "maternal mortality" figures always *include* deaths from induced abortion, ectopic pregnancies, appendicitis, trauma, etc. and therefore they must necessarily always be higher than abortion deaths alone.

In the United States, Dr. Sachs took up Dr. Beral's term and reported from the Center for Disease Control, Atlanta, Georgia: "By 1975 pregnancy prevention was responsible for nearly as many deaths as pregnancy itself."[25]

PHYSIOLOGICAL LIVING

The sensible conclusion to be drawn from the disasters listed above is that we should stick close to Nature and live in a physiological fashion. This applies particularly to marriage, childbirth and family limitation. With the passing years we come to admire more and more the genius of the design of the Creator. My motto in medicine, *a fortiori* in obstetrics, is: "The physiological is the optimum." In other words, it is impossible to improve on the normal function. Therefore one should try, in the absence of disease, to live without medication or interference in bodily processes. However, the philosophy of the modern medical profession tends towards over-treatment, especially in obstetrics where rates of induction of labor commonly run up to 50 percent. This borders on the absurd, what is called in medicine *furor operandi* (a craze for operating).

For example, the Caesarean rate in the United States increased from 5.5 percent (which should still be considered a normal figure) in 1970 to 24.7 percent in 1988. If this was the median figure, the top figure in the range must have been about 40 percent.[26]

With great wisdom Aristotle (d. 322 B.C.) once said that: "Any drug given to a healthy person must necessarily do harm and cannot do

25. Sachs, B.P., *et al.* "Reproductive Mortality in the United States." *J. Amer. Med. Assn.* (1982), *247*, 2789-92.
26. Taffel, S.M., *et al.*; also Myers, S.A., *et al.* (Letters). "U.S. Cesarean-Section Rate." *New Eng. J. Med.* (1990), July 19, 199-200.

good." Yet we see in the contraceptive field millions of healthy women taking large amounts of sex steroids and inevitably causing harm to themselves. It is similar to the craze among male athletes to take anabolic steroids to build up their muscles and improve their performances. This foolish policy sometimes leads to early deaths, or to unusual fractures, and as time goes on it seems almost certain that the personality is affected and violent behavior is seen. For example, in 1990 at the World Police Medical Officers Conference, a Harley Street forensic physician related several such cases. One fanatical British body-builder on steroids raped three women and murdered another. Another murdered his infant son. A third, aged 27, died of liver hemorrhage caused by drug-induced tumors. Note the similarity to the effects of the sex steroids (OCs).

When they reach the age of about 50, innumerable good husbands and wives come to realize how blessed they have been simply through following the design of the Creator in marriage and sexuality. They have enjoyed normal intercourse, they have not risked avoidable health hazards, their larger families have forced discipline and fidelity on them, their marriages are secure against any stress, and their children provide endless interest and fulfilment in what might otherwise have been rather empty lives. Being faithful to God and Church fosters grace and spiritual strength, and at the same time protects them from harm.

NATURAL FAMILY PLANNING

This leads on to a consideration of NFP and it should be obvious logically that, since all other methods of contraception are morally flawed, there is really no choice. For those who perceive the issues clearly, the only method which is licit and blameless is NFP. This should cause no surprise as it is, of course, God's design of the reproductive system. Creation, which was initiated eons ago, is still a continuous process. The whole of Nature moves in pulsating rhythms, gigantic in the celestial sphere, more modest in the terrestrial. The seasons follow one another inexorably as the planet Earth spins in space, tied by invisible bonds to Brother Sun while gentle Sister Moon, remote but familiar, watches silently over us.

A similar rhythm is impressed on human affairs, especially in the working of the reproductive system. The menstrual cycle is the evidence of the rhythmical fluctuation of fertility and sterility throughout the month. Menstruation itself fosters the concept of a rest from sexual activity for one quarter of each cycle. The psyche of the woman lets her know instinctively that the norm in marriage must be times of activity followed by rest. (Pity the poor "modern" woman on D.-P. who has complete absence of menstruation and must be available for intercourse every day of the year!) The Creator has designed mankind for eight hours of sleep and the daylight hours for work; for six days of work and for rest on the seventh. And we depart from this pattern at our peril.

Ecclesiastes (3:1-8) expresses the same idea: "There is a time for every purpose under the sun . . . a time to be born, a time to die . . . a time for loving, a time for staying apart. . . ." And this is the essence of NFP, times of sex alternating with times of abstinence. This may sometimes be onerous but, if it is adhered to throughout married life, it brings an elemental satisfaction and many unforeseen benefits.

This is not the place for a detailed instruction in the use of NFP, but the general principles will be explained. In most cities there are now NFP clinics run by a handful of doctors, nurses and lay instructors. An extraordinary phenomenon is the almost complete rejection of NFP by the medical establishment. Ask any medical student what he thinks of NFP and he will immediately reply that it is no good, it doesn't work, etc. He does not know a thing about it, but his teachers have told him that it is used only by a small group of religious zealots. Moreover, it requires a certain degree of abstinence and sexual control and, in a sex-obsessed society, that is quite impossible. *Finis.*

There is probably a deeper philosophical reason for the modern attachment to artificial contraception and the rejection of the natural, and that is an instinctive realization that the two concepts of sexuality are antipathetic, mutually exclusive. NFP is essentially pronatalist while the artificial methods are antinatalist. Opting for NFP would logically oblige one to reject not only contraception but also sterilization and abortion, and that is a sacrifice which most weak and confused doctors are unwilling to make. Will they open their arms to Nature, espouse physiological living without recourse to drugs or devices? Never!

HOW NATURAL FAMILY PLANNING WORKS

The wife is fertile for about one day in each month (the duration of viability of the ovum, which is released at ovulation); the husband is fertile every day; the husband-wife combination is fertile for about six days each month (assuming five days of viability for the sperm and one for the ovum). But in its practical application nine days of abstinence should be advised (seven days before ovulation and two after it). The reasons for this caution are that the vitality of the sperm cells varies in each male, and the environment within the vagina and cervix ranges from "hostile" to favorable in its effect on sperm movement. As there are no laboratory tests which would refine the diagnosis more precisely, the best policy is to assume maximum vitality of the sperms in each couple, especially if they have demonstrated a high degree of fertility in previous years. Many authors assume a five-day sperm survival time as the maximum, but I have always recommended seven days of abstinence before ovulation. I am convinced from clinical experience that most failures of this system are caused by a too optimistic reduction of this pre-ovulatory period. Moreover, given the fallibility of the human condition and the vagaries of love, it is a safer policy to prescribe a strict formula than a lax one.

The key variable in applying the NFP method is therefore ovulation, and most of the effort is directed towards timing, or diagnosing, or detecting this event. It is extraordinary that the ordinary housewife in her home can diagnose ovulation with as much accuracy as the biochemist in his laboratory. The diagnosis is based on several independent observations. One of the most interesting is the changes in cervical mucus discharge day by day throughout the cycle. This method has been refined over the years by the pioneering work of a unique medical couple, Drs. John and Evelyn Billings, of Melbourne. They have shown that illiterate Third World women can easily interpret the dynamic changes in the normal vaginal discharge and successfully use the NFP system.

Another remarkable researcher in this area is Professor Erik Odeblad, of the University of Umea, Sweden, but most gynecologists are unaware of his research. It is common knowledge that the mucus discharge from the cervix at the time of ovulation becomes profuse, translucent, less viscous and more able to be drawn out into threads (*Spinnbarkeit*). Odeblad has been able to show that there are different types of mucus, that they are produced at different levels of the canal in the cervix, and that the microscopic fibrils of glycoprotein in the mucus change their character day by day. At ovulation the mesh of fibrils opens sufficiently to allow the sperms to penetrate; but at other times the mesh closes up and prevents their access into the uterus, hence the "infertile" days.

Other simple but accurate indicators of ovulation are the morning temperature record (basal body temperature - BBT) and ovulation pain (*Mittelschmerz*). In my opinion this latter observation has been largely neglected by NFP writers, but it is a precise timer of ovulation and it is easily recognized by most women once its significance has been pointed out to them.

With these various techniques ovulation can be diagnosed at the time or in retrospect — but only the mucus observations, either its presence in various forms or its absence, have any predictive value. For perfect clinical results, we need a prospective sign or symptom up to seven days before the occurence of ovulation. So far, this has not been achieved. It is only highly fertile couples who are disadvantaged by this deficiency. Despite all these qualifications, the NFP system is very satisfactory as a method of family limitation and as a way of life.

EFFECTIVENESS OF NATURAL FAMILY PLANNING

How effective is the NFP system in avoiding pregnancy? It has suffered from a bad press, not only in women's magazines but also in the medical journals, especially in articles written by contraceptive doctors. Presumably they have a vested interest in giving this dog a bad name. It is not uncommon to read FPA (or IPPF) articles claiming pregnancy rates for NFP of 20, 30 or even 40 per 100 woman-years. These figures are almost beyond belief. To put them in perspective, the pregnancy rate of women trying to conceive is never more than 80. A witch doctor chanting imprecations could probably report results in the 20-40 range.

There are no profits to be made when people use NFP because it is a simple uncomplicated way of life, but if women use conventional contraception each client becomes an investment because she must be seen every few months for years ahead. Is this judgment too cynical? If so, apologies!

My first article on this technique was in 1956, some four years before the OC was introduced, and my results at that time, using only the old calendar method ("rhythm") were fairly good. In 156 patients the total pregnancy rate was 5.0 per 100 woman-years; and the method failure rate (that is, when patients followed the instructions properly) was only 3.3. [27]

In 1975 [28] I published a further series of 600 patients with a total pregnancy rate of 4.7 and a method failure rate of 2.7. On this occasion the patients were selected on the basis of proven fertility, that is, they must have had a pregnancy either before or after inclusion in the series. This requirement is seldom demanded in contraceptive studies. It has the disadvantage of producing less impressive effectiveness rates, but it is the only honest way of making a true assessment.

Many women are sterile but do not realize it. For example, to take only one sterility factor, unsuspected tubal blockage is often present in those who have used IUDs, or had induced abortions, or follow a promiscuous life style. They could not get pregnant if they tried. It is easy to see how such subjects are invaluable in any contraceptive study, because they contribute many years of apparent successful use and thus minimize the pregnancy rate in a misleading way.

The only genuine way to assess any contraceptive rechnique is to eliminate secondary and unsuspected sterility, that is, by requiring the subjects to have achieved a pregnancy *after* using the contraceptive. This, of course, drastically reduces the number of women on the series and also makes for higher pregnancy rates.

I have come across only two articles where the patient selection was made on this basis, one of them being by me. [29] The effectiveness of any method of family limitation cannot be expressed as a simple

27. Dunn, H.P. "The Safe Period." *Lancet* (1956), Sept, 1, 441-442.
28. Dunn, H.P. "Natural Family Planning." *N.Z. Med. J.* (1975), *554*, 407-408.
29. Dunn, H.P. "The Reliability of the Safe Period." *Aust. N.Z. J. Obstet. Gynec.* (1966), *6*, 331-34.

percentage figure, e.g. 97 percent effective, as this assessment makes no allowance for the time factor. The standard formula involving both time and numbers of subjects involves the number of pregnancies per 100 woman-years. This was devised by Raymond Pearl, the notable American researcher in the 1930s. In recent years this has become "couple-years," to emphasize that in the NFP system the fertility depends on both partners in the marriage. The standard to which all methods are compared is the effectiveness so often claimed for OCs, that is, one pregnancy per 100 woman-years.

Many of the claims for record-breaking low pregnancy rates must be accepted with a certain amount of scepticism. In series involving Third World countries or with tens of thousands of women, the follow-up is unlikely to be accurate. In fact, many of them would never be seen again, or they might be pregnant or even dead. In many reports the "average duration of use" is only about 13 months — but in the latter months the women might be in early pregnancies; or be sterile from breastfeeding; or cultural abstinence might be imposed.

Another factor encouraging caution is the regrettable modern phenomenon of fraud in scientific papers. It is therefore essential nowadays to determine what is the moral quality of the author being quoted. For example, Caton[30] stated that: "Fraud is not being detected (only) in institutions of low repute, but (also) in the laboratories of eminent scientists holding appointments at prestige institutions." A man's ethical philosophy must be consistent in every area. There have been some notable modern instances of top politicians who have abandoned their wives for younger and more attractive women, but they have had to resign from their key government posts. The unspoken judgment of the otherwise amoral community is that, if a man is unfaithful to his wife, he might be unfaithful to his country. Moreover, the elements of the antinatal triad are now billion-dollar industries. Any adverse reports will prove costly to all concerned, whereas there is no money to be made out of persuading people to adopt the no-equipment, physiological sexual practice which NFP involves. A man who espouses the injustice of abortion is unlikely to be aflame with the justice which demands the truth.

30. Caton, H. "Truth Management in the Sciences." *Search*, (1988), *19*, 242-244.

One of the few admissions of higher failure rates with OCs is found in an unlikely source. [31] The writer, quoting a book by L. Potter, stated that more than 63 million women worldwide use OCs, which represents about 8 percent of all married fertile women. While claiming that failure rates ideally are less than one percent, in practice they "are often much higher . . . as high as 20 percent. . . . The primary cause of high failure rates appears to be incorrect use."

As successful use of the OCs demands a certain degree of behavioral discipline and determination, it is not surprising that failures are common among teenagers. This is one of the reasons why sex education in schools leads to an increase, not a decrease, in teenage pregnancies. On the one hand the girls are given the impression that casual sex is the norm, and on the other they are not sufficiently sophisticated to be consistent pill takers. Another conclusion to draw from this admission is that it is quite irresponsible for a doctor to tell a patient with a serious obstetric problem that she must go "on the pill" and then she will be "perfectly safe."

NFP has a sliding scale of "safety" depending on the accuracy of the detection of ovulation and the span of the days of abstinence. Those in whom pregnancy would be hazardous should restrict intercourse to the days after ovulation and not use any days following menstruation.

Professor Thomas W. Hilgers, of Omaha, Nebraska, has shown that, when NFP is applied properly, pregnancy rates of less than one per 100 couple-years can be achieved. The "use effectiveness" figures, which is adversely affected by human error, is about five. [32]

Case Report

Several years ago I had a patient who had six children, each one a failure of a different contraceptive technique — pill, condom, withdrawal, diaphragm, spermicide, douching. I said to her, "Why

31. "The importance of oral contraceptive compliance." *IPPF Medical Bulletin*, (1990), *24*, 2-3.
32. Hilgers, T.W. "We need good NFP Doctors." *All About Issues* (1990), May, 32-33.

don't you try the NFP method?" She said, "Oh no, I wouldn't feel safe!"

It was hard not to laugh. But she was a good little woman and the children were charming. It is to be hoped that they never found out about their origins.

ADVANTAGES OF NATURAL FAMILY PLANNING

It remains only to list the advantages which people who use NFP enjoy. Often these are not appreciated until many years of married life have passed. Good young couples who keep to NFP for philosophical or religious reasons sometimes envy their friends and relations using modern contraceptives, imagining that they have continuous access to blissful sex with never a thought about pregnancy. But this promised Garden of Eden often proves to be an illusion, and the conjugal couch is by no means always a bed of roses.

1. Normal intercourse is preserved. NFP shares this advantage with hormonal contraception and IUDs, but there the similarity ceases.

2. The method is esthetically and morally acceptable to people of all races and all religions. This should cause us no surprise, as it is obviously the design of the Creator and therefore it must be perfectly adapted to all human beings.

3. No drugs are used, therefore there are no inherent dangers in the method. Modern society has gradually become aware of the health hazards involved in permanent medication of healthy young women or in any interference with the normal physiology of the body. This naturally appeals to those in back-to-nature and ecology movements.

4. Once the method has been learnt, there is no cost involved and no equipment is needed. This is important for all young people, but especially for those in Third World countries.

5. The responsibility for family limitation is shared equally between husband and wife. With all other methods one or the other partner assumes the complete responsibility, and in the majority of marriages

this unfortunate partner turns out to be the wife. She is permanently taking OCs or having hormone injections: or she has an IUD acting as a foreign body within her uterus; or she is constantly applying a diaphragm or spermicidal medications within her vagina — all for the sake of providing sterile intercourse as required. The common pattern of life is that, after a few years of this, she gets fed up and demands a sterilizing operation either for her husband or for herself.

With NFP there is an equality of sacrifice, therefore neither partner feels that he or she is being used. There is no denying that, as the marriage ceremony says, sacrifice is always difficult and irksome, but love will make it easy and perfect love will make it a joy.

6. Self control is fostered. Control of sexuality is unpopular in a licentious world, but it is an inescapable duty for everyone. If a man can discipline his sexual nature, his life must be counted a success.

Undisciplined sexuality, fostered by alcoholism and pornography, is a major cause of modern social disruption: spirituality dies, violence erupts, there is infidelity both before and after marriage, divorce flourishes and families are split up. The children suffer more than do the parents.

NFP forces sexual discipline on the spouses. However unwelcome this may be, they gradually realize that their marriage is secure if illness or separation brings an abrupt halt to their intimate love. Each has demonstrated repeatedly to the other that he, or she, is able to control the imperious demands of sexuality. Fidelity may never be mentioned, but it is guaranteed.

It is a very different situation in marriages which have never had to deny themselves access to intercourse. Their serenity is immediately compromised, and only outstanding characters will be able to cope with this test of love. Those who live by the sword will die by the sword; and those who live by sex must suffer the penalties of sex.

7. NFP is not detrimental to the unmarried. This may seem an odd thing to say but it is to point out the evil of the reverse situation, that is, the harm done to the young through their access to contraceptives. Sex education in the schools is mainly contraceptive instruction, and the young are not slow to use them. If they are instructed in NFP at all, it is

mainly information about the signs and symptoms of ovulation, and the message that abstinence is of the essence.

8. Those who use NFP seldom or never progress to abortion. As explained above, by a mysterious but perverse logic, those who use contraception eventually come to accept sterilization and then abortion, because they are all manifestations of antinatalism.

FOUR QUESTIONS

Is NFP a good system? Yes.

Is it a perfect system? No. There is no such thing in the world of contraception.

Is it the best system? Undoubtedly.

Is it the only system? Yes. There is no alternative for those who live by love and purity and justice.

CHAPTER 4

Sterilization

ENDLESS vistas of carefree sex with not the slightest risk of an inconvenient baby popping up on the horizon — that is what sterilization offers. But, while it admittedly produces many satisfied customers, the reality is often less than idyllic. There is a fateful finality about the decision to accept sterilization; it is really turning one's back on childbearing forever.

In recent years sterilization has increased markedly in popularity, so much so that in the United States it is claimed that possibly between 25 and 50 percent of young marriages are now permanently sterilized. It is difficult to arrive at precise figures, but at least we can be sure that tremendous numbers of marriages are sterile. And the performance of Catholic couples in this area is quite as bad as that of their friends who have no religious guidance at all. I remember once seeing a reader at Mass struggling painfully up the sanctuary steps to the lectern. Only I knew that she had had a sterilizing operation a fortnight before, a prize example of the unfaithful faithful Catholic.

According to a survey of 8,400 women of childbearing age in the United States, reported by the National Center for Health Statistics and also Brown University, 43 percent of Catholic couples have been sterilized, made up of 22 percent of Catholic women and 21 percent of Catholic men. (Quoted by *The Wanderer*, May 31, 1990.)

These figures, and similar ones for contraception and abortion, reveal the massive rejection of papal teaching by ordinary Catholics and probably the absence of sound teaching from their pastors.

The usual pattern of reproductive policy for most Western marriages is: 10 years of contraception and abortion which results in about 2.0 children per marriage; then the wife becomes annoyed with carrying this antinatalist burden on her own, realizes that there are at least another 10 years of fertility ahead and opts for sterilization of one or the other partner. In happy marriages this decision is often made on truly compassionate grounds but in others it can be a cause of contention, especially where a domineering wife persuades a reluctant husband to submit to surgery. Sexual bliss is not automatically achieved through this operation.

This huge loss of fertility might have national significance if a country ever realized that it was facing demographic disaster from the falling birth rate and sought to increase its population. It would be an impossible project. If the Ministry of Agriculture were to report that half the sheep and cattle in the country were sterile, it would be regarded as a national crisis. But the fertility of human beings is looked on as more of a curse than a blessing, and the government keeps on subsidizing the sterilization of its citizens as they rush down the Gadarene slope into extinction.

A. FEMALE STERILIZATION

In the female, the standard procedure is division and ligation (tying) of the Fallopian tubes, hence the colloquial "I've had my tubes tied." The often imperfect perception of the nature of the operation is illustrated by the patients who say: "Doctor, I've had my tubes tied. Now I want them untied." Unfortunately, the situation is not as simple as that.

The common procedure is now laparoscopic sterilization — the tubes are approached through a tiny incision at the navel, a lighted telescope is inserted and the target organs are divided, or a clip (or band) is placed on them, or their whole length is destroyed by diathermy. Bands and clips are out of favor because their failure rates are too high.

Sometimes the tubes are divided through a vaginal approach, especially if there is some degree of prolapse (dropping of the uterus) which makes the operation easy. But the laparoscopic and the vaginal operations have the advantage of needing only a one-day hospital stay.

Are there any *dangers* with these operations? While they are usually very safe operations, it would be foolish to imagine that any surgical procedure or anesthetic is quite without risk. The worst thing that could happen is death, and this risk is greater with those patients who have a serious medical problem.

Laparoscopy looks like a simple operation but there are some unexpected hazards. In one of my wards there were once three patients with laparoscopy complications — one had a hole in her bladder, one a hole in the large bowel, and the third had had an injury to the iliac vein. At a clinical meeting in the same hospital, two deaths associated with laparoscopy were reported. The first step in the operation is to inflate the abdominal cavity with gas, usually carbon dioxide. Gas absorption can disturb the blood chemistry. And if the intra-abdominal pressure goes too high, it can obstruct the blood flow in the great vessels and lead to malfunction of the heart.

A rare but dramatic complication is an intra-abdominal explosion, which is an embarrassing contretemps for all concerned. If the bowel is accidentally pricked, methane gas escapes and when the diathermy is switched on to destroy the tubes — bang!

Puerperal Sterilization

The puerperium (the days immediately after childbirth) is the worst, not the best, time to have any operation. The only advantage is convenience, making one convalescence serve for two illnesses. About one quarter of all mothers are now being sterilized within a day of having their babies, while they are still exhausted, dehydrated and depressed. At this time the clotting mechanism is operating at its maximum level, and any operation might precipitate a pulmonary embolism (clots passing to the lungs, sometimes fatal).

Years ago I even saw a patient who had a hernia repaired after her delivery; and another had her varicose veins operated on! This is truly tempting Providence.

Fortunately some leading hospitals are now abandoning puerperal sterilization, not only because of the anesthetic and clotting risks but also because the patient might later change her mind; or the newborn baby might unexpectedly die; or it might show up an unsuspected abnormality.

Parallel with the boom in sterilization is another surgical bonanza — the increasing demand to have the operations reversed. This is now so common that many surgeons plead with their sterilizing colleagues to use techniques that make reversal easy! They are especially annoyed with the gynecologists who destroy the whole length of the tubes with diathermy. This absurd situation reveals a certain degree of confusion in the minds of both doctors and patients. "Yes, Doctor, I'm absolutely certain that I want to be made permanently sterile. But I don't want it to last forever. I may change my mind after a few years. That's a woman's privilege."

As a practical proposition, an operation to reverse sterilization is not to be undertaken lightly because the chances of success, that is, pregnancy, are only about 15 percent. With microsurgery in the best hands better results have been reported, but there is always the risk of a later serious complication, ectopic pregnancy (in the tube). For most women a sterilizing operation must be regarded as permanent and irreversible.

Reasons for Sterilizing

These operations are performed to avoid future childbearing hazards for either mother or babies. Even unmarried girls are some-times sterilized if there seems to be a bad prognosis in pregnancy, an hereditary disease or mental retardation. This serious surgical decision should always call for a second opinion. That is the patient's main safeguard.

The commonest "indication" for sterilizing is simply multiparity, that is, having a large number of children. But of course, the figure commonly accepted to qualify for that adjective is a purely arbitrary one. A few years ago eight was considered a "large" family; now four is regarded as unconscionable.

In 1950 Prof. William Dieckmann, of the Chicago Lying-in Hospital, the then doyen of American obstetrics, came to the conclusion that "the risks of sterilization are greater than those of undisturbed fertility," and therefore "sterilization for multiparity alone cannot be justified on medical grounds." Nothing has changed in the intervening years to make that opinion any less valid.

Other indications for sterilizing, and incidentally for wanting the patient not to embark on another pregnancy are: high blood pressure, severe diabetes, heart disease, kidney failure, psychiatric breakdowns, and so on.

Repeat Caesarean Sections

A special note must be made about this common dilemma because it is almost routine to find patients being sterilized at the time of the second Caesarean. The abdomen is opened, it is very convenient, so why not? This reveals the sentimental approach to surgery — the operator obviously feels that it is too much to expect the patient to have a third Caesarean, or a fourth.

It may be a burden, but it is not an impossible one. In many cases the operation is surprisingly easy and may take only about 20 minutes. In fact, some patients say they would prefer an abdominal delivery to the pain and difficulty of the normal process; but, although one can understand the reason for this preference, the vaginal route is always the optimum one unless there are some serious complications.

There are two main problems which worry the obstetrician when dealing with a patient who has had one or more previous Caesareans. Are there dense adhesions which will make access to the lower segment of the uterus difficult? And, is the previous uterine scar weak and likely to rupture at the end of pregnancy or in labor? There are no diagnostic methods which can help him. He has no way of finding out apart from inspecting the area during the operation. Some patients are such "good healers" it is sometimes difficult to see the scar after even four Caesareans; in others the scar may be dangerously thin after only one.

As modern obstetricians trained in the sterilization era have no personal experience of the strength of the uterine scar, it is necessary to go back to older medical writers for this clinical information. Dr. Fleetwood Churchill, writing in 1872 (sic.), stated: "Further, on a good number of these patients, Caesarean section has been performed more than once; on some three and four times. And, if we credit the older writers, we find five, six and seven times with success."[1]

McNally[2] reported 130 patients having four or more Caesareans, surely a unique series. Of these, 84 patients had 4 Caesareans each; 30 had 5; 9 had 6; 5 had 7; one had 9; and one had 10.

He stated: "The results of this series make one conclude that the capabilities of uteri subjected to repeat Caesareans are underestimated and that the majority of scars, even in advanced parity, remain intact."

They quoted Dr. Robert Cosgrove of the Margaret Hague Hospital, Jersey City, which at that time was the largest maternity hospital in the United States. Referring to sterilization after two or three Caesareans, Cosgrove said: "such practive is medically archaic . . . there should be no set limit, provided the integrity of the uterus is maintained."

Feeney[3] described a patient who had 10 Caesareans. "During an obstetrical life of 20 years the patient enjoyed good health and survived the ministrations of four successive Masters of the Coombe Lying-in Hospital, Dublin. . . . It is considered that nine Caesareans and then one Caesarean-hysterectomy (for ruptured uterus) may constitute a record."

One of my colleagues in a country practice had a Maori patient who had 10 uncomplicated vaginal deliveries following a Caesarean in her first pregnancy. The Caesarean had been a "classical" operation, that is, with a vertical incision in the body of the uterus. This type of scar, which is seldom seen nowadays, has always been regarded as more dangerous than the modern transverse (lower segment) scar.

1. Churchill, F. *On the Theory and Practice of Midwifery*. Henry Renshaw, London. 1872, p. 409.
2. McNally, H.B., *et al.* "Patients with four or more Caesarean sections." *J. American Med. Assn.* (1956), *160*, 1005.
3. Feeney, J.K. (Correspondence). *British Med. J.* (1954), Dec. 11, p. 1421.

Case Reports

I myself have had a number of patients with multiple Caesareans. In reporting on 3,000 private patients, I had 136 Caesareans (incidence 4.5 percent, which is an indication of conservative management; in the United States at present the national average incidence is 20 percent). Of my cases 29 had 2 Caesareans; 14 had 3; 8 had 4; 4 had 5; and 2 had 6.[4]

These two latter cases both had Caesarean-hysterectomies because their uterine scars were so thin that they would not take a needle and therefore could not be sewn up from superior to inferior. They could be sewn only from side to side, after removal of the uterus above this level. Ideally the cervix should be removed at this operation, but in pregnancy the bleeding is sometimes so heavy that this additional surgery becomes difficult and dangerous.

In ordinary gynecological practice, hysterectomy is often performed — for menstrual problems, painful periods, malignancy, fibroids, cervix abnormalities, and so on. If a patient came with an abnormally scarred uterus, it would be quite licit to remove it. But it is not licit to operate on normal tubes (direct sterilization).

Remote Complications

There seems to be widely accepted misapprehension, that, once a patient has been sterilized, that is the end to all their sexual and childbearing problems. Nothing could be further from the truth. Coping with post-sterilization remorse and disappointment is a growth industry for psychiatrists and sociologists.

1. *Failure*, that is, pregnancy, is the first surprise. The failure rate is at least one percent; I have seen a seven percent figure quoted. These figures are worse than can be achieved by simply using the pill or natural family planning.

4. Dunn, H.P. "3,000 Personal Obstetric Cases." *N.Z. Med. J.* (1970), *72*, 308-310.

One of my surgical colleagues, a first class operator, had an extraordinary experience in this area. He sterilized a patient and she later become pregnant. After the delivery he sterilized her again. She became pregnant once more! After this delivery he did a hysterectomy.

Fortunately this was in the days before induced abortion was legalized. Now the routine response to this situation is to offer the patient an abortion to compensate for her disappointment, not to say rage. This, of course, is still quite illegal as "failed sterilization" or "failed contraception" is not an accepted indication. But "psychological stress" is.

Another factor may be that, particularly in the United States, pregnancy from failed sterilization is often the basis for a huge claim for damages. Nobody dares to mention these hidden thoughts of the gynecologist, but the casual observer might come to the conclusion that throwing in a free abortion makes more economic sense than paying out on a million-dollar baby claim. Would any member of this noble profession sacrifice his intrauterine patient to save himself a million dollars? Regrettably, the answer in some cases is: Yes.

Not surprisingly, doctors tend to publish in the medical journals only their best results. Therefore, the risk faced by the average patient is always worse than the reported figures. And the pregnancy incidence must rise with every passing year. It is therefore important always to know what the duration of the follow-up is. In an unpublished series from one of my hospitals (it has an excellent professional reputation), the duration of follow-up was only 12 months or less. But during this time, of 446 patients who had vaginal tubal ligations, 1.6 percent were already pregnant. And of 434 who had laparoscopic sterilizations, 1.4 percent became pregnant. Hardly reassuring figures.

Many people cannot understand how these failures occur. One ridiculous explanation is: dividing the wrong structure, that is, cutting the round ligament instead of the tube. That is why surgeons now are advised to send a section of the presumed tube to the pathologist for his confirmation that this was the right tissue!

The commonest cause of failure is the mysterious tendency of any tubular organ, after being blocked or divided, to recanalize, that is, to reopen its former cavity. This applies not only to the divided tubes but also to the vas (in males), to arteries, to varicose veins and to hernial sacs (producing a recurrence of hernia). In the reproductive area one can romanticize about the irrepressible life force which is so hard to extinguish despite man's best (meaning worst) efforts.

2. *Ectopic Pregnancy.* Fertilization, the start of the new pregnancy, takes place in the tube and within the first week it moves down into the uterus where it becomes implanted. Occasionally it gets stuck in the tube, the pregnancy slowly enlarges and after about a month it suddenly ruptures with bleeding into the abdominal cavity. The patient experiences a severe pelvic pain and often faints.

There has been a marked increase in ectopics since 1970 and this emergency, formerly rare, is now seen every week in gynecological hospitals. This raises the question: what happened about 1970 which could account for this increase?

Dr. Valerie Beral, a noted English researcher, believes that the ectopic explosion must be attributed to the following factors: the great increase in sterilizing operations; the introduction of IUDs; and the use of new progesterone-only oral contraceptives, all of which enjoyed a boost about that time. The National Center for Health Statistics in the United States, when reporting a four-fold increase in ectopics between 1970 and 1987, added another causative factor: "the increased occurrence of pelvic inflammatory disease resulting from sexually transmitted disease" — what used to be called venereal infections, the price these unfortunate young women pay for promiscuity. [5]

In case an incorrect impression is given by these facts, it should be pointed out that many women of undoubted virtue, eschewing both contraception and sterilization, also feature among ectopic cases. There are other causes which are difficult to explain, such as the ovum from one side getting into the tube on the other side.

Ectopics are now a leading cause of maternal mortality. Cases are sometimes reported where the husband comes home from work and finds his wife dead on the floor.

5. "Ectopic Pregnancy - United States, 1987." *Morbidity and Mortality Weekly Report,* June 22, 1990. *39*, 401-404.

Case Report

> *I was on emergency duty and was called to the hospital to see a very ill patient. She had been sterilized six months before, and on the day of admission had collapsed. She was pallid, had a distended abdomen and was exquisitely tender to touch. Within a minute I was able to tell her she had an ectopic and needed an emergency operation.*
>
> *"How do you know? Are you sure?" she said.*
>
> *"I knew before I ever saw you," I replied. "The registrar told me you had been sterilized, your period is a week overdue, you had a sudden severe pain and fainted. It couldn't be anything else. Ectopics are a well recognized complication of sterilization."*
>
> *"Why wasn't I told?" she asked.*
>
> *I was unable to answer.*
>
> *At operation she had to have a transfusion of six packs of blood (about 3,000ml.). She was lucky to survive.*

3. *Menstrual Disturbance.* Another curious complication of sterilization is the development of menorrhagia (heavy periods) after the operation, and therefore many of the patients come to hysterectomy — two operations instead of one. (Or, for prudent women, none.)

Even though this complication is widely recognized and has been reported in the medical literature for over 40 years, it is still difficult to prove. Menstrual abnormality is often a very personal assessment, many women complaining about losses which are really slight while others put up for years with "flooding" because they think every woman behaves as they do.

Advocates of sterilization claim that the menorrhagia phenomenon is explained by the fact that after the operation the women stop taking their oral contraceptives which themselves have created only a scanty menstrual loss. This does not seem to be an adequate explanation. There may be an anatomical explanation — the operation may interfere somehow with the unusual arterial loop between the ovarian arteries and the uterine arteries, and this may influence the menstrual loss. Another observation is that there may be gross dilatation of veins in the infundibulopelvic ligament (draining from the ovaries and uterus), but once again this is difficult to prove. An editorial comment is interesting:

"In one series almost 20% of women who had been sterilized had to undergo hysterectomy within 10 years; while Chandler found that half of a group of women aged under 45 who had hysterectomies had already been sterilized."[6]

It is easy to see how this subject does not lend itself to precise statistical analysis. For example, after sterilization the uterus is perceived by the patient as "a useless organ," therefore why put up with any menstrual abnormality for the next 10-15 years? Better to get rid of it. And for the surgeon there may be a financial inducement as well.

B. MALE STERILIZATION - VASECTOMY

This seems like a simple little operation which can be performed under local anesthesia, just a snip-snip excision of part of the vas which conveys the sperm cells from the testicle to the seminal vesicle (storage sac) and then no further worries about pregnancy. But, as is so often the case, things are not quite as simple as that. The sperm cells stored in the seminal vesicle are not eliminated until there have been several ejaculations. Therefore the surgeon requires the "liberated" male to masturbate for him at interval until he finds that all the sperms have gone, whereupon he gives the patient the green light to sexual freedom.

Failure

Once again the vas, like the tube, has a tendency to recanalize and failure (pregnancy) occurs. It always seems insulting to the baby to describe his arrival as a "failure" but that is the trend in modern sexual philosophy.

The highest failure rate I have seen is a colossal 5.3 percent, and that was at the hands of a group of specialist sterilizers, Vasectomy

6. "Hysterectomy and sterilization: changes of fashion and mind." *British Med. J.* (1977). 17 Sept., 715-716.

Services Incorporated (sic) of Cincinnati.[7] The authors stated that the common failure rate for vasectomy was between one and two percent.

The great increase in male sterilization in the past two decades is almost incredible. Prior to this it was always the females who were sterilized, probably because the burden and hazards of childbearing impacted mainly on them. There must be a deep philosophical reason for this change of emphasis. Obviously the women have revolted against carrying the whole responsibility for contraception and sterilization, and one must sympathize with these unanticipated victims of the sexual revolution. (If only they had stuck to Judeo-Christian ethics in marriage and used natural family planning, where husband and wife share the burden equally. . .) Now the female worm has turned and sent the emasculated male off to get "fixed up." The modern emancipated (which means promiscuous) male gets what he deserves.

Remote Complications

It is hard to imagine how much a minor operation could have any serious sequelae, but once again the principle is thrust into our minds that there is always a price to pay for any interference with Nature (in this case, operating on normal organs). When the vas is tied off, there must be a damming-up effect for the sperm cells which continue to be produced in the testicle. This seems to lead on to some degree of protein resorption, and this in turn reacts adversely on the immune system. One rare complication is therefore arthritis of the small joints of the hands and feet. In vasectomy experiments in monkeys there seems to be a disturbance of cholesterol metabolism and a progressive blockage of the coronary arteries, but it is difficult to prove that human subjects have an increased incidence of coronaries.

Walker[8] followed 6,092 vasectomized men and found that there was a small increased risk of subsequent prostate problems, but he

7. Kaplan, K.A., *et al.* "A clinical study of vasectomy failure and recanalization." *J. Urology* (1975), *113*, 71-74.
8. "Hospitalization Rates in Vasectomized Men." Walker, A.M., *et al. J. American Med. Assn.* (1991), *245*, 2315-7.

could come to no definite conclusions about coronaries or arthrius. He noted in passing that some 150,000 vasectomy operations are being performed each year in the United States!

Even the hormones are affected by vasectomy. This is a probable explanation for the fact that, even if men have a technically successful reversal operation, their fertility still remains low. Fisch[9] found that there was an increase in antisperm antibodies in 52 percent of men after vasectomy and this led on to an increase in various pituitary hormones (produced in the brain).

Another extraordinary and unexpected risk is stressed by Cale.[10] He found that the incidence of testicular tumors in Scotland has risen in the past decade parallel with the increase in vasectomies. The risk seems to have risen by a factor of 4.2. He stated, as suggested above, that "immunological and pathophysiological effects have been shown to occur after vasectomy."

An even more surprising hazard after vasectomy is the possibility of urolithiasis (kidney stones). In studying 11,205 vasectomized men, Kronmal stated: ". . . we found a highly significant relation between vasectomy and renal disease."[11] The relative risk for later calculi (stones) was multiplied by a factor of 1.67; and in the younger age group (30-35 years) the relative risk figure was 2.6. They estimated that the annual number of vasectomies in the United States was one million!

In an editorial expressing concern at the vasectomy explosion, Hussey[12] noted that ". . . increasing numbers of men have had the operation, and for some it has become a status symbol (!)" Furthermore, ". . . other authors have warned that, aside from immediate postoperative complications, vasectomy may be followed by psychosocial aberrations or autoimmune response disorders."

9. "Detection of Testicular Endocrine Abnormalities and their Correlation with Serum Antisperm Antibodies in Men following Vasectomy." Fisch, H. *et al. J. Urology* (1989), *141*, 1129-32.
10. "Does vasectomy accelerate testicular tumour? Importance of tesucular examinations before and after vasectomy." Cale, A.R.J., *et al. British Med. J.* (1990), *300*, 370.
11. "Vasectomy and Urolithiasis." Kronmal, R.A., *et al. Lancet* (1988). *1*, 22-23.
12. "Vasectomy - a Note of Concern: Reprise." Hussey, H.H. *J. American Med. Assn.* (1981). *245*, 2333. (Editorial)

Psychosocial Implications

This inelegant adjective indicates that, after sterilization of either husband or wife, there are sometimes serious problems ahead either in the area of interpersonal relations or in society at large.

Sexual performance is such a sensitive business that it is easily deranged by unanticipated psychological factors. It is difficult to apply standard medical assessment to this private section of life, but it would be safe to assert that sexuality is optimal when the two partners are locked into a happy marriage where there is complete trust and fidelity and where love expresses itself in a generous solicitude for the happiness and pleasure of the other lover. This idyllic situation, which I have encountered in thousands of my good patients, is not likely to be found among the sterilized group.

It is not surprising to hear that some of the husbands suffer from varying degrees of impotence; or they may go to the other extreme. But the promised sexual bliss often eludes them.

Some years ago (1979) there was a report from the Hammersmith Hospital, London, on 103 women who, during the space of 16 months, attended the clinic and asked for reversal of their sterilizations. Dr. Winston remarked that "sexual dissatisfaction after sterilisation was common," and many of the marriages broke up. He concluded that: "It therefore seems unwise to sterilise women under 30, particularly immediately after pregnancy, or if their marriages are in jeopardy." Wise words that have been completely ignored by his colleagues in later years.

Social workers often note an increase in marriage breakdown after sterilization. There is now in society a large pool of vasectomized men who, in some cases, are a menace. (Not your husband, gentle reader, but all those other sexually liberated bounders.) It is not good for a man to know that he has a guarantee of sterility. And regrettably the same applies to some of the ladies as well. The result is that infidelity is encouraged and has now reached epidemic proportions.

Sterilization is sometimes as much an obsession with the doctors as with the patients. This is shown by the fact that it is only a small proportion of the doctors who generate the majority of the operations. Strange to say, some lady gynecologists perform enormous numbers of sterilizations, so much so that they become an action picture of their own sexual philosophy. The only good sex is sterile sex. Sometimes it seems that the whole of the hospital organization has jumped on the bandwagon. Whenever a woman is having her 4th + baby, or her 2nd + Caesarean, she has sterilization pressed on her by the doctors, the nurses, the medical students, the clinic staff, even the wardsmaids. It is both an obsession and an impertinence.

Management Blunders

The first blunder is the failure to convey to the patient the realization that, from the practical viewpoint, this operation must be accepted as irreversible. Only a tiny minority will be able to get access to and afford the microsurgery which may restore the patency of the tubes or vasa.

Who can foresee the future? A patient in my city had her tubes tied after her fourth baby. Not long afterwards, her husband and all the children were killed in a car accident. A few years later she remarried and bitterly regretted her inability to have more children. As she realized, too late, the childbearing difficulties of the time were only temporary. And moreover fertility is a precious gift, not a curse.

Another serious blunder which is never publicized in the medical journals is for the husband to rush into vasectomy, but a short time later the wife has to have a hysterectomy for some genuine gynecological indication, such as fibroids, or malignancy, or heavy bleeding. This stems from the failure to view fertility as a function of two partners, not simply one. The husband comes to realize that he has had an unnecessary operation and also that he has permanently lost his fertility. The shortest interval I have encountered between vasectomy and subsequent hysterectomy was three months; and I have heard of a one month interval! But the surgeons enjoy a financial bonanza.

If a pregnancy should occur in a vasectomized marriage, and if the partners are generous enough to give the new baby a welcome, there is often an excited time of congratulations and exclamations about "the miracle." But it appears to be ungracious to remark, as Sherlock Holmes would have done, that "There might be another explanation for the facts, my dear Watson." Statistically the chance of an old-fashioned interloper are greater than those of a miracle. In charity one ought to keep those thoughts to oneself, but if they do occur to the husband they could provide the scenario in which both spouses regret ever having decided on sterilization. Once again the wisdom of Holy Mother Church is confirmed.

C. MORAL ASSESSMENT

This is the heart of the matter. If sterilization is wrong in all circumstances, it may not be performed and all the pragmatic arguments listed above are of no juridical importance. Thanks to the lack of ethical teaching in society and the confused principles of most of the Christian churches, few people have a clear outlook on the issue. Many feel that there is something not quite right with sterilization but they cannot articulate it, and moreover even if it is wrong, serious circumstances may justify it — "the end justifies the means." This is the common fallacy which dominates Western society, even though St. Paul in Romans 3:8 teaches the exact opposite: you may not do evil that good may ensue.

In essence sterilization is a mutilation because it destroys a normal functioning organ. Many people do not see it as such. How can a little operation like this, a tiny incision like this, be a mutilation? And performed by such a nice doctor? And all our friends having it done? Preposterous!

The true nature of the operation is seen when we consider punitive (penal) sterilization or genocidal sterilization. The first group have the operation inflicted on them as a punishment. Castration (removal of the testicles) is a related mutilation aimed at reducing the activities of sex offenders.

In India compulsory sterilization of the peasants was a major factor in the 1978 defeat of Mrs. Gandhi's government. Even though they were impoverished, the peasants valued their fertility and they fought against the armed police who came to take them off to the hospital by force. And it should be remembered that Hitler at one stage had a policy not of killing but of sterilizing the Jews, gypsies and psychiatric patients.

Depriving these groups of their fertility was an expression of contempt and hatred. Is it any different for a compliant patient?

Direct sterilization is forbidden by the Fifth Commandment, "You shall not kill." This Commandment forbids not only homicide but also suicide, mutilation, cruelty, violence, and careless disregard of health (by drug addiction, alcoholism, dangerous driving, wilful spreading of disease such as AIDS, and so on).

This Commandment was obviously given by the Creator for all mankind. Like all divine laws, it must of its nature be for the benefit of human beings and of society, even if with their myopic vision they cannot see this in the short term.

If anyone had any lingering doubts as to the immoral nature of sterilization, he need only listen to the teaching authority of the modern Popes who have consistently condemned it.

Pope Pius XI in *Casti Connubii* (1930) pointed out the sinful nature of self-mutilation in general and of compulsory sterilization in particular. At this time the Nazis were about to embark on their genocidal policy.

In 1951 Pope Pius XII stated: "Direct sterilization — that is, that which seeks as a means or an end to render procreation impossible — is a serious violation of the moral law and is therefore illicit.

"Even the public authority has no right, on the plea of any indication, to permit it and much less to employ force, to the prejudice of innocent beings. This principle is already asserted in the encyclical of Pius XI concerning marriage.

"Hence, when some ten years ago sterilization began to be ever more widely applied, the Holy See found it necessary to declare expressly and publicly that direct sterilization, permanent or temporary [this definition would include oral contraception], whether of the man or the woman, is illicit by virtue of the natural moral law, from which the Church herself, as you know, has not the authority to dispense." (Address to Italian Catholic Midwives)

In his encyclical, *Humanae Vitae* (1968), Pope Paul VI confirmed this teaching: "Equally to be excluded, as the teaching authority of the Church has frequently declared, is direct sterilization, whether of the man or of the woman." (N. 14)

No-one could ask for clearer teaching than that, but in the modern world thousands of Catholic patients, hundreds of Catholic doctors and dozens of Catholic hospitals have embraced sterilization. Is this because of confusion or cowardice in the face of the enemy, or simply rejection of the authority of the magisterium? There are plenty of "liberal" (meaning laxist) theologians causing confusion among the "faithful." And cowardice has a long tradition among Christians, starting with St. Peter and the others who abandoned Christ during His Passion, and extending down to the present day, this writer not excluded. As Malcolm Muggeridge once said, our motto seems to be: "Backward, Christian soldiers." But not all have been traitors. There have been thousands of martyrs, and "the blood of martyrs is the seed of the Church" (Tertullian, c. 180 A.D.). The holy women who ministered to Christ, St. Veronica who wiped His bleeding face, and His Blessed Mother were notable exceptions. Their courage should be an inspiration to modern women.

CHAPTER 5

Abortion

"WHAT greater pain can mortals bear than this: to see their children die before their eyes." Euripides (d. 406 B.C.) The great Greek dramatist was mistaken. He could not have foreseen that 24 centuries later women would be flocking to have their children destroyed on a scale never before seen in the history of the world, 50 million of them dying year after year through abortion. It has an impact on human society so great that it makes the atomic bomb seem like a simple firecracker.

Abortion, along with the other antinatalist procedures described above, may eventually lead to the demise of Western civilization. The populations of all these countries are now static, and soon they will begin to decline at an ever increasing rate. Besides destroying society abortion is also destroying the family, the timorous medical profession and particularly my own specialty.

Obstetrics and gynecology are now mainly in the hands of the abortionists. No decent young doctor would want to enter them, but even if he did the difficulties would be almost too great. Junior staff in most of the training hospitals are expected to do their share of abortions. Standing out against the tide calls for innumerable personal acts of courage, but this is what the profession has failed to do — and therefore it has lost its reputation for nobility and independence.

The doctors rationalize their dereliction of duty to the unborn child like this: Abortion is now legal; we have a duty to see that the law operates properly; we hate abortion but we must give the mothers the best techniques available; furthermore, if we don't do it, they will just go to some backstreet abortionist and suffer dreadful injuries.

This stance is riddled with fallacies. Very few countries afford a blanket legality to abortion, even though in practice it might be "abortion on demand." An unjust law does not bind. And their excuse of acting under the duress of the law finds an exact parallel in Shakespeare's great bloodthirsty drama, *Richard III*. Richard had thrown his brother, the Duke of Clarence, into the Tower of London and then hired two thugs to kill him.

> *Clarence*: The deed you undertake is damnable.
> *First murderer*: What we will do, we do upon command.
> *Second murderer*: And he that commanded is our king.
> *Clarence*: Erroneous vassals! The great King of kings
> Hath in the table of His law commanded that
> Thou shalt do no murder. . . . (I, iv, 195)

The doctors likewise plead that they are acting under the command of Parliament. Mistaken slaves of society! The great Commandment, "Thou shalt not kill (the innocent)," still applies to all mankind.

Poor Clarence, the fratricidal victim who had himself arranged a few murders, was stabbed and then drowned in a butt of malmsey wine. A pity to waste so much good wine.

THE FETUS

The debate on abortion is unending and confusing, but it is useful to confine any discussion to two main issues: What is the fetus? And, what is abortion?

There is no doubt that from the time of conception, the fetus is a new, unique and separate human being. He may not look very attractive, but his anatomy and physiology are perfect for each particular stage in development. The various terms used to describe him (fertilized ovum, morula, embryo, fetus, baby, child, infant, etc.) are merely matters of scientific convenience. From conception the new life starts; it is then that he receives the chromosomal genetic endowment from each parent. All that is needed is time and nutrition to allow him to develop into the appealing newborn child whom everyone loves.

These are simple facts of embryology. Yet we see in the modern scientific world attempts to change the facts — doctors who claim that life does not begin until implantation about two weeks after fertilization. Dame Mary Warnock's Committee on *in vitro* fertilization recommended that life should not be seen to start until day-14, the purpose being to allow for either early experimentation on the embryo or for abortion if any abnormality was suspected. Doctors should not be influenced by such specious argumentation.

In fact, it is precisely IVF that confirms the fact that life begins at conception. When they achieve fertilization and they have a one-cell or a two-cell human being, that is the time that the IVF practitioners and their patients break out the champagne and congratulate one another. By a curious anomaly, the new life has begun but the mother is not yet pregnant! But, those considerations aside, they don't say: "Wait until implantation, because there is not yet any living organism." Or, "Wait until the child achieves personhood," whatever that means. "Personhood" is a neologism which is useful in denying the child the right to life if the doctors plan to abort him.

It is not generally realized that the facts outlined above are confirmed by Scripture. Since this is the inspired word of God as St. Paul points out, we are obliged to believe it despite pseudoscientific protests. (2 Timothy 3:16) It is all in the first chapter of St. Luke's Gospel. Christ first featured in human history as an embryo — at the time of the Annunciation. There was no question about His life starting a fortnight later. The Redeemer was already in the womb of the Blessed Virgin. She then went "with haste" to visit St. Elizabeth. From this simple phrase we can deduce that she did not put off her Visitation for a fortnight or a month. She would have had to arrange to go with a caravan; and then moving at donkey pace, the long trek from Nazareth to Ain-Karim near Jerusalem would have taken about five days.

When she arrived Elizabeth, inspired by the Holy Spirit exclaimed: "Why is it granted to me that the mother of my Lord should come to me?" The point of this story is that she knew that the embryo in Mary's womb was already her Lord. There was no question of saying that He would be that later in the pregnancy. Or that He would have to wait to achieve "personhood" before being honored by her prayer. And then Mary confirmed Elizabeth's perception of her true status by launching into her wonderful *Magnificat*:

"My soul magnifies the Lord,
and my spirit rejoices in God my Savior,
for He has regarded the humility of His handmaiden.
For behold, from henceforth all generations will call me blessed:
for He that is mighty has done great things for me,
and holy is His name. . . ."

Her prediction has proved to be true — now almost 2000 years later, we still call her the Blessed Virgin.

Of course it is easy for patients, and even for some doctors, to convince themselves that what the uterus contains in early pregnancy is not a human being, but in a scientific world we must be logical and believe the evidence of our senses. If they are uncertain they have only to wait a few weeks or months and they will then see the familiar and undeniable human fruit of pregnancy.

WHAT IS ABORTION?

Our whole discussion is, of course, focused on induced abortion, not on accidental abortion (miscarriage) which involves no moral issue. It is common for pro-life advocates to show photos or slides or tapes of abortion procedures, but I am not convinced of the wisdom of portraying these horrors, even as shock treatment. Suffice to say that, however abortion is dressed up as a brilliant technique and ingenious anesthesia, it still remains cruel, ruthless and barbaric. And in the end it brutalizes all involved, doctors, nurses and patients.

This is what the profession and the legislators have opted for.

First trimester (three months) — the usual procedure is suction curettage. The small and fragile fetus is sucked out of the womb by a powerful vacuum and in passing down the narrow curette it is dismembered, limbs torn from the trunk and the head pulled off the body. One theatre nurse is detailed to make sure that she can count two legs, two arms, one head and parts of the thorax. If she is careless these tiny parts are sometimes passed at home a few days later.

Second trimester — as the fetus is larger suction curettage cannot be used, but some operators develop skill in the D & E procedure (dilatation and extraction). Working blind within the cavity of the uterus, he fractures the baby's spine, decompresses the skull by suctioning out the contents, and if the cervix is sufficiently dilated the trunk can be removed without further dismemberment.

Much more common is the intrauterine injection of hypertonic (super-strength) saline solution, which burns the skin of the baby and kills it by a complex biochemical effect.

After a day or two the uterus starts in premature labor and delivers its already necrotic burden. "Man's inhumanity to man."

An alternative procedure in dealing with the larger fetus is the operation of hysterotomy, which is really like a miniature Caesarean section. The tiny baby is lifted out of its warm home and left to die from prematurity and asphyxia. As every woman knows, there is often some uncertainty about the maturity of any pregnancy, even with the help of ultrasonic assessment. Therefore these late abortions often produce babies which could survive with good pediatric care. Some years ago there was a notable case in Glasgow where such a baby was discovered crying weakly among the hospital's garbage. In the legal prosecution which followed, the judge ordered that in future such cases must have a pediatrician available so that resuscitatory measures could be undertaken if the child was born alive. This is, of course, the height of absurdity — one doctor attempting to kill the child and another trying to save its life. In fact, in this case the aborting doctor's defence was that his unwritten contract with the patient was for a dead baby, not a live one, and therefore resuscitating it was "inappropriate." And the Medical Association and the various Royal Colleges and their ethical committees say nothing about this gross dereliction of duty.

In the United States, where obstetricians are constantly in danger of million-dollar lawsuits, there is the additional financial stimulus to produce a dead baby. The patient would be very annoyed to find that she had a live baby and that she would have to pay for perhaps three months of care in a neonatal unit. American doctors openly call this "defensive medicine."

The reality of this situation, which only a few years ago would have been almost unbelievable, is illustrated by two landmark prosecutions of aborting doctors. In Boston, a doctor who was performing a hysterotomy opened the uterus and instead of delivering the baby he hooked the cord out with his finger, cut it and stopped the operation while the baby bled to death. In the other case, a Los Angeles doctor achieved a vaginal delivery of the premature baby, but, as it was alive and kicking and crying, the nurses placed it in a cot in the nursery. When the doctor was notified, he ordered all the staff out of the nursery and about ten minutes later told them that the baby was dead. The autopsy findings of fracture of the larynx and cricoid cartilage, as well as bruises on the neck, proved that he had strangled the child with his bare hands. Both cases came to court on homicide charges and in both of them the jurors' verdict was "Not guilty." The jury spoke for society, the profession and government — what they all want is unrestricted access to abortion, even if it means the garbage dumps are littered with tiny human bodies.

This is well illustrated in my own country. In 1977 Parliament passed the Contraception, Sterilisation and Abortion Act. (Note the acceptance of these three elements as a linked triad — so much for the common spurious claim that contraception is a prophylaxis against abortion. They are actually symbiotic bedfellows.) Parliament thought it was going to do what no other government in the world had done, namely, to enact legistlation that would control the abortion monster, not realizing that once the first abortion is officially permitted the floodgates are opened. As we predicted, the abortion rate soared. Doctors sanctimoniously record the "indication" which is assumed to justify the abortion, and in 97 percent of cases this is "a threat to psychological health." This, of course, is beyond the bounds of reason. And, although the politicians presumed that every abortion would be done for a medical reason, in practice the standard greeting to the new pregnancy patient is: "Do you want it? Or do you want an abortion?" It's as simple as that.

RU 486

The most significant develoment in the abortion field is this drug which produces the "do-it-yourself" or "home" abortion. It is an antiprogesterone substance which interrupts the implantation process in early pregnancy, producing a medical type of abortion. But it is not quite as simple as originally stated. It is an inescapable principle that any interference with a normal pregnancy must involve some risk. In fact the patient must attend her doctor at least three times, sometimes more; and there is always the chance that she will need a subsequent curettage, just as with any spontaneous miscarriage.

Nevertheless, the prospects of an escalation in the already rocketing abortion rate are very real. One must admire the Americans for enterprise and direct action. While most of us would be sitting at home and wringing our hands, Dr. Jack Willke, head of the national right-to-life organization in 1991, took the fight right to the home of the RU 486 manufacturers, Roussel Uclaf. He led a delegation of leading Americans and religious leaders to the factories in Frankfurt, Berlin and Paris with the "information" that they represented over 100 million Americans, and that if RU 486 were introduced into the United States they would organize a massive boycott of Roussel Uclaf pharmaceuticals and take other unspecified measures. Willke commented laconically that the manufacturers "got the message."

DISPOSAL

The sordid nature of abortion is highlighted when it comes to disposing of the tiny human corpses produced by the faithless parents and the unfeeling surgeons. In the United States there have been numerous accounts of hospital dumpsters filled with hundreds of fetuses or their dismembered parts, waiting to be taken to the city refuse dump or incinerator. Others have been sold for profit.

"We now have a flourishing commerce in the sale of fetal tissues and organs, such as that at the Hana Biologics Institute in Berkeley, California . . ." said Dr. Bernard Nathanson in *New Dimension Magazine* (October, 1990).

Hana proposes to supply fetal pancreas tissue for diabetics, brain tissue for treatment (probably ineffective) of Alzheimer's Disease and Parkinson's Disease, bone marrow, skin, corneas, livers and other organs for transplantation.

Two journalists, Litchfield and Kentish[1] gave us the first exposé of the barbaric rackets involved in the British abortion industry. They mentioned, among other nauseating details, the sale of fetal fat to cosmetic manufacturers. It seems that for producing high-class facial creams there is nothing to equal the fat of very young human beings.

To show that there is nothing new in the field of barbarism take this quote from a newspaper in 1890 (sic):[2]

"A series of crimes of the most horrible nature (a correspondent of *La France* says) has been discovered at Constantinople. A barber, aged 70, and his wife were long in the practice of alluring (sic) to their house young persons whose *embonpoint* (plumpness) suited their purpose.

"These they killed, and with their fat, when boiled, composed an unguent (ointment) which was sold at a high price. When discovered by the police they were in the act of cutting up a plump Armenian boy of 10 years of age.

"Both miscreants, after a short interrogatory, were hung up at their own door."

The similarity of these various projects to cannibalism is obvious, but anyone who supports or legislates for abortion cannot logically profess shock at these crimes against humanity.

All these horrifying examples prove that the child suffers in the modern philosophy of sexuality and becomes an object that can be bought or sold or used at the whim of its parents. In the cause of sexual freedom the lives of millions of our fellow human beings are ended. They were, we must assume, conceived in love, formed in the image of their Father in Heaven, destined for immortality — but then their brief lives end, their bodies discarded, dismembered, burned, unwanted, unremembered, unbaptized.

---

1. Litchfield, M. and Kentish, Susan. *Babies for Burning.* Serpentine Press, London (1974).
2. *New Zealand Herald,* June 26, 1890.

RISKS OF ABORTION

One of the catchcries of the Abortion Law Reform Association is: "Safe, legal abortion." This is a delusion. Abortion, any operation, any anesthetic, always carries some risk, even if small. There is a significant mortality rate for the mothers and a 100 percent rate for the babies. The immediate risks are: hemorrhage, infection and perforation of the uterus, even in the hands of experienced surgeons. The operator is working "blind" within the cavity of the uterus; and in pregnancy the wall of the uterus is so soft that it is fatally easy to perforate with the curette. These complications sometimes necessitate hysterectomy as an emergency measure. I have come across scores of reports of hysterectomies in teenagers. Before the abortion era these blunders and tragedies were never heard of.

If any readers are sceptical about the risks women face in "safe" abortion, perhaps they will believe Dr. Henry Morgentaler, Canada's leading abortionist who operated in defiance of the law for many years but who in the end, almost single-handed, forced legalization on that country. Credit must be given him for his persistence, even though the legislative decision has proved disastrous for the nation. The Consent Form used in his Toronto abortion clinic reads (in part):

"I have been informed that complications of this procedure [abortion], such as allergic reaction [presumably to anesthesia], perforation of the uterus and intestines, hemorrhage, infection, infertility, hysterectomy and error in estimating duration or existence [!] of pregnancy, while rare, may occur, and I accept this risk. . . . " Note the ever-present hazard of having the womb removed in an emergency, usually life-threatening operation. And the admission that sometimes the "abortion" is performed when the patient is not even pregnant.

The remote risks are: sterility, incompetence of the cervix, Rh sensitization, and uterine rupture in a subsequent pregnancy. Sterility is caused by infection, even if minor, at the time of the abortion — but the patient is unaware of the situation until she tries to conceive, perhaps years later.

Rh sensitization is not so common as it used to be, but it still occurs. The trauma of the abortion procedure sensitizes the mother and any subsequent baby is affected, sometimes in a serious fashion which defeats treatment such as intrauterine blood transfusion of the child. Therefore all later babies die in the womb or soon after delivery.

The traumatic dilatation of the cervix during late abortions sometimes disrupts and damages the cervix to such a degree that it cannot "hold in" later pregnancies, and therefore a succession of prematures are born with all their inescapable hazards such as spasticity, visual defects and so on. We had one such case who had four mid-trimester miscarriages following her abortion, despite having Shirodkhar sutures placed round the cervix (circlage) and also intravenous tocolytics (drugs which damp down uterine action).

If the uterus suffers an undetected perforation at the time of the original abortion, this leaves a weak spot which might rupture suddenly during a subsequent pregnancy or labor. I saw one such case who collapsed at 24 weeks; the baby was half extruded through a rent in the top of the uterus and was already dead. She had to have an immediate hysterectomy.

Note that in all these cases described, the baby which the mother discarded in the initial abortion proved to be the only one she might have had. None of these unfortunate and misguided women will ever have another baby — but these tragedies, which are repeated hundreds of times, never feature in any medical statistics. In fact, the original abortions would all have been recorded as "successful" cases. Many of the disasters in life go unrecorded but, if only these distressed women had understood and kept to God's law, none of these devastating experiences would have happened to them. But in the excitement of the Sexual Revolution and the distress of the unexpected pregnancy, this message is hard to get across.

HIPPOCRATES AND ABORTION

Abortion has always been with us because for some women pregnancy has always been burdensome, or embarrassing or dangerous. The oldest legal system to penalize a citizen who caused an abortion was the Sumerian Code (c. 2000 B.C.). In the Assyrian Code (c. 1500 B.C.) the fetus was referred to as a human life, and there was a penalty for taking it. A similar concept is found in Exodus (21:22-23): "If men fall out and one of them strikes a woman who is pregnant, so that the child is stillborn, but she herself lives, he must pay whatever sum the woman's husband demands and the judges agree; if her death follows, then life must pay for life."

The great Greek physician, Hippocrates (d. 377 B.C.) formulated his famous Oath which for 24 centuries has been accepted as the touchstone of medical ethics — but in this century for the first time the profession has rejected his teaching. One section of the Hippocratic Oath, which all medical graduates used to take, states:

"I will follow that system or regimen which, according to my ability and judgment, I consider for the benefit of my patients, and will abstain from whatever is deleterious or mischievous. I will give no deadly medicine to anyone if asked, nor suggest such counsel; and in like manner I will not give to a woman a pessary to produce abortion. With purity and holiness I will pass my life and practice my art. . . ."

Note how he associates euthanasia with abortion. They are both offspring of the same anti-life monster. It is an undisputed observation that all abortionists favor euthanasia; and all of those who practice euthanasia are in favor of abortion. This is why modern medical schools either drop the Oath or administer a watered-down and ambiguous version.

Hippocrates carries no juridical or ethical authority, but his importance lies in his demonstration of the noble standards which can be achieved by the good pagan relying only on the natural virtues of love and justice. If only modern Christian society could equal this nobility!

REASONS FOR ABORTION

If we are to combat the evil of abortion, we should attempt to understand the basic reasons for this sociological phenomenon and work out our defence in a rational manner. But huge global movements are often difficult to explain. It is like fashion; someone in Paris decides on, say, short skirts or long skirts and by the start of the next season the message has been diffused all round the world. Nothing can stop it, no matter how absurd the style might be.

Abortion seems to be a global death wish with all nations, oriental or occidental, rushing lemming-like to destruction. It is reminiscent of the ancient pagan god, Moloch, who is referred to in the Old Testament. The mothers used to bring their infants to the statue, place them on his outstretched hands and from there they would be dropped into the flames. A similar crazed lust for human sacrifice was found among the Aztecs before the conquistadores came to Mexico. On the top of the huge pyramids of the Sun and of the Moon close to modern Mexico City 1000 young people might be sacrificed in one day, their hearts torn out and offered to the Sun God. Abortion is child sacrifice to Sex.

Abortion can also be seen as a form of civil war, our own citizens killing their fellows in the womb. And, as everyone realizes, civil war is the most bitter form of all, brother hating brother and never suing for peace.

Another significant concept is that abortion is one facet, indeed the final victory, of the Sexual Revolution which has swept through society during the past 50 years and has gained its biggest boost from the introduction of oral contraception in 1960. The essence of the Revolution was to free women from the burdens which they felt society had unfairly laid on them — freedom from pregnancy, from marriage, from monogamy, freedom to have sex of every variety with anyone of either gender, freedom from menstruation, from their anatomy and physiology, from every decent thing that made up a real woman, a lady. And, of course, freedom from being called "a lady" which they now regard as the ultimate insult. It is obvious that abortion is essential in this scenario, given the fallibility of modern contraceptives and the almost invincible power of human fertility in the design of the Creator. The FPA calls it "backstop" abortion, hoping to give the impression that anyone who has a knowledge of cricket can't be all that bad.

On the other hand, it is important to see what abortion is not. And that is: a therapy for illness. Abortion has nothing to do with health. That means, if all abortions were stopped tomorrow, there would be no deleterious effect on either personal or national health. I made this point years ago in a major article on "therapeutic" (a misnomer) abortion[3] in

3. Dunn, H.P. "Theraputic abortion in New Zealand." *N.Z. Med. J.* (1968), *68*, 253-258.

which I reviewed the world literature through over 60 references and concluded that there are no medical indications for abortion.

In fact I shall repeat here a challenge I made in one of my first pamphlets on abortion, a challenge that was never taken up by any abortionist, even though it would have given him an easy money prize. This offer is for anyone who still holds that there are medical indications for abortion; or, put in another way, that abortions are performed for medical reasons. I will put up $1,000, the abortionist $100, that is, he will enjoy 10 to one odds, and all he has to do is produce three consecutive abortion cases in which the medical "indications" were incontrovertible. If it was only one case there might be interminable disputes, the clinical situation being sometimes simply a matter of opinion; but three cases make it a matter of sincerity. If the abortionist takes up the challenge, he is a fool; if he does not, he is a hypocrite. The judge could be a mutually chosen professor of obstetrics and gynecology.

DIABOLICAL ORIGIN OF ABORTION

I am now convinced that the basic cause or genesis of the abortion plague is a diabolical one. Nothing else could account for such massive injustice, the slaughter of the innocents on such a huge scale. Satan, the Prince of Darkness, has an obsessive hatred of the innocent. When Christ was on Earth he hated Him since He was the epitome of innocence and holiness. But now that He has returned to His Father the next most innocent available target for Satan is the child, both born and unborn. All those involved in abortion are agents, often unwitting, of Satan.

We have all been in that situation at one time or another, because we have all sinned with the sole exception of the Blessed Virgin. If we reject Christ, we ally ourselves to Satan. But in all our faults, especially abortion, there is often so much confusion and duress that clear consent of the will may be lacking and therefore culpability may be minimal or even absent. If abortion is therefore a spiritual malaise at base, it must be tackled at that level, that is, through prayer and penance.

MORAL ASSESSMENT

Considered objectively, abortion is the direct killing of an innocent human being. Every word in that definition is important.

"DIRECT" — the assault is directly on the unborn child. Sometimes in medicine the child dies indirectly from therapy of unrelated organs and an accidental miscarriage takes place, for example, when there may be radiotheraphy of a cancer, say, of the ovary or the cervix. Or possibly from an anesthetic and operation for appendicitis. There is no moral fault in these circumstances, but it is easy to imagine some borderline cases where "the benefit of the doubt" must be given to the doctor and to the patient.

"KILLING" — is the real aim of the exercise, as has been shown in some late abortion problems. But it is unwise, possibly unjust, to use the word "murder," even though it may sometimes be literally true. "Homicide" is a better term.

Among the vast numbers of women who have been through the abortion tragedy there are always some who later come to help the pro-life struggle, and these tortured women often say that one of the things that had made their conversion difficult was being labelled as a "murderer." The approach to all women in this agonizing dilemma must therefore be one of open arms and true compassion. Unless, of course, she happens to be hitting you over the head with a placard on a stick and screaming obscenities. In those circumstances charity can wait. Just run for cover.

"INNOCENT" — the child in the womb is often described as an unjust aggressor against its mother, but this is stretching imagination too far. The baby did not ask to be conceived. It is incapable of volition or aggression. It merely happens to be in this particular situation at an inconvenient time.

"HUMAN BEING" — as we have seen, there is no question but that it is a new human person right from conception. It is not "a parasite on the mother," or "a tumor" which can be removed. It is not "a few cells," or "a piece of tissue," as the abortionists so often describe it to their pathetic clients. Or they say: "A woman has the right to do what she likes with her own body." Her own body! This is almost invincible ignorance. What we are speaking about is not her body but her child's. All that her body does is to give it shelter and sustenance for nine long months, after which all normal women then give it love and a lifetime of care.

Another pro-abortion catchcry along similar lines is: "Woman's body, woman's choice." And, as a derivative of that line of thinking, a person who favors abortion describes herself as "pro-choice," the implication being that she approaches the problem in an enviable democratic fashion, while the benighted pro-life peasants have no choice, being enslaved by their consciences, their churches and the oppressive Law of God.

Once again we have the obfuscation caused by harping on about the woman's "body" rather than her child. There is also the common statement that abortion is women's business and it should not be decided by male politicians or doctors. But the whole question is one of justice, the taking of the life of an innocent unborn person, and men are equally competent with women in making this decision. In fact, despite all the rhetoric, none in this *dramatis personae* has really any choice. The child is protected by God's Commandment, "You shall not kill," and that is the end of the matter.

This discussion reminds one of the oft-quoted statement in Deuteronomy about another fateful choice: ". . . this day I set a choice before you, life or death, a blessing or a curse. Will you not choose life. . . .?" (30:19) The life or death drama is as old as human history and, given man's perverse capability, he so often in the past has chosen death.

The killing of the innocent unborn child is always wrong, whatever the circumstances. This is an absolute prohibition set out in the Fifth Commandment: You shall not kill. This is not a Catholic, or a Christian, or a Jewish commandment. It was given by God to Moses and through him to the whole human race, both before his time and since. The obligation to protect innocent human life rests equally on all men, of all religions and of all ages. Christ, the perfection of innocence, was in danger from Herod as soon as He was born; now children are hated both before and after birth.

Since the earliest times the Christian Church has consistently condemned abortion as murder, yet now we witness the spectacle of certain clergy serving on the executive of the Abortion Law Reform Association, and some church hospitals offering the very best "safe, legal abortions."

In the *Didache* (c. 100 A.D.) there is a command: "You shall not kill the fetus by an abortion." Athenagoras (177 A.D.) and Tertullian (225 A.D.) both described abortion as murder. Similar statements were made by St. Cyprian (d. 258 A.D.) and St. Hippolytus (d. 235 A.D.) and also by the Council of Elvira (300 A.D.)

St. Basil the Great (d. 375 A.D.) stated: "A woman who deliberately destroys a fetus is answerable for murder. And any fine distinction as to its being completely formed or unformed is not admissible among us." In the 5th century St. John Chrysostom, St. Augustine and St. Jerome all held similar views.

In the modern world abortion has been condemned repeatedly in papal encyclicals and allocutions, and in a reply from the Holy Office.

This constant teaching was confirmed by the Second Vatican Council. In *Gaudium et Spes* (The Pastoral Constitution on the Church in the Modern World), n. 27, it states: "Furthermore, whatever is opposed to life itself, such as any type of murder, genocide, abortion, euthanasia, suicide . . .; all these things and others of their like are infamies indeed."

Again in n. 51: "Therefore from the moment of its conception life must be guarded with the greatest care, while abortion and infanticide are unspeakable crimes."

Many good people are horrified by abortion but they make exceptions in cases of rape, or incest, or suspected fetal abnormality. This stance is philosophically indefensible. It is also sentimental, and it reveals that its supporters are opposed not to abortion *per se* but only to a great mass of abortions, on the grounds that the end justifies the means. This is the common error on which the whole of Western society has foundered. It was condemned by St. Paul who stated explicitly that we may not do evil that good may ensue. (Romans 3:8) The prohibition of abortion is therefore absolute.

Many people have the impression that it is only the Roman Catholic Church that rejects abortion in all circumstances, but this is not absolutely true. Admittedly the Catholics perceive the issues more clearly than do their friends in other religions, and they have the advantage of unequivocal and infallible guidance through the papal magisterium — but there are untold numbers of good people of all religions who daily seek to do the right thing and keep the Commandments of God according to their own personal judgment of the issues.

For example, we recently saw an Open Brethren patient who had a cancer of the cervix diagnosed during pregnancy. She refused abortion or any treatment of the malignancy until the baby was delivered. This is the modern equivalent of the courage of the martyrs. If she had acceded to the advice re abortion, she would have lost her baby and there was no guarantee that she herself would survive. She was willing to risk her life for the sake of her child. This acted out the scenario so eloquently described by Our Lord: "Greater love than this no man has, that a man lay down his life for his friend [or child]." (John 15:13)

But it is undeniable that the confused teaching of other leading Churches has led to the abortion disaster that afflicts society today. In 1965 at the start of the abortion civil war, the Anglican position was expressed by the Church Assembly Board: it sanctioned abortion if there were medical indications.

The National Council of Free Churches adopted a similar stance. The liberal Jewish view was equally permissive, according to the late Dr. Alan Guttmacher, of New York, President of the International Planned Parenthood Federation, the largest contraceptive and abortion organization in the world. He added: "It was only after the firm establishment of the Protestant Movement that medically indicated interruption of pregnancy was given religious, ethical and legal sanction by any Church group." This reveals the real, and apparently insurmountable, difficulties which confront the ecumenical movement.

Jewish acceptance of "legal" abortion is a distressing fact of life. Israel has one of the highest rates of abortion in the world, the ratio of abortions to births being at least 1:2, possibly as high as 1:1. Therefore the national birth rate is below replacement level, while that of the Druse Arabs is very high. While Israel is fighting for its national life militarily, it is destroying itself from within through its antinatalist policies. This anomalous situation cannot continue indefinitely. It is hard to imagine that, after four or more millennia, the Chosen People will commit race suicide, but that is exactly what is happening.

On the other hand, an Orthodox Jewish view was expressed by Dr. Immanuel Jakobovits, Chief Rabbi in Britain: "Based on these principles, present day rabbis are unanimous in condemning abortion, feticide, or infanticide to eliminate a crippled being, before or after birth, as an unconscionable attack on the sanctity of life."

Some comfort can be taken from orthodox statements by leading Protestant divines in the recent past.

Dietrich Bonhoeffer, the great Lutheran theologian who was murdered by the Nazis in 1945, wrote in his *Ethics*:

"Destruction of the embryo in the mother's womb is a violation of the right to life which God bestowed upon this nascent life. To raise the question whether we are here concerned with a human being or not is merely to confuse the issue. The simple fact is that God certainly intended to create a human being and that this nascent human being has been deliberately deprived of his life. And that is nothing but murder."

Professor Helmuth Thielecke, of the University of Hamburg: ". . . once conception has taken place it is no longer a question of whether the persons concerned have responsibility for a *possible* parenthood; they have *already become* parents."

Professor Karl Barth, of Basle, came to the conclusion: "He who destroys germinating life kills a man."

Acceptance of the fact that the child in the womb has an inalienable right to life is a further test of faith in the modern world, but sadly so many fail that test. Espousing abortion is evidence of weakness of faith, and it is often the final step in a long human saga which ends in the abandoning of all religious practice. But this ought not to be an excuse for despair. The power of grace is unlimited, and there have been innumerable examples of people who have regretted their wrong decisions and turned to their loving Father in Heaven.

WHAT TO DO

The pro-life organizations, the politicians and doctors often appear frantic in their efforts to stop the juggernaut car of abortion which is crushing everyone in its path. Or it seems like a tidal wave of hedonism, a tsunami, which is sweeping round the world and crashing over helpless people. It will be a long struggle. It has been working up for a century, and it may take a further century to fade away into the mists of history. It is therefore a battle with no end, but one we must never give up because we are fighting for justice.

The first thing is to recall people to the concept of the unborn child as having an inalienable right to life. And taking his life in abortion is gross injustice. From the time of conception he is a new human being with an immortal soul and an eternal destiny. He is already a child of God and he has been redeemed by the blood of the Savior. He is our brother and we must protect him from harm.

The next thing is to join a pro-life organization because this battle cannot be fought by individual soldiers. It is only through large organizations that we can hope to influence the all-powerful politicians.

Of course it is essential to help distressed pregnant women with every practical help we can muster. It is not sufficient merely to "counsel" them. They need endless friendship and support.

Education of the community about the nature of the fetus and of the abortion process is an important duty. It is amazing how much knowledge we now have about the developing child from the one-cell stage right up to birth. The heart is already beating at the 6-week stage and it will continue working day and night for the next 70 years or more. Ultrasound scans show that he is moving within the womb for at least two months before the mother feels the "quickening." The womb is a noisy place with a sound level of over 85 decibels, which is equivalent to that in a factory or in the cab of a diesel truck. The baby hears the beating of his mother's heart (Is this why humans have an instinctive sense of rhythm?), bowel sounds, and the resonance of her speaking and singing. Incidentally, this shows up the absurdity of the modern fad of delivering the baby into a room with dim lights and only whispered sounds.

In dealing with young audiences I doubt the wisdom of shocking them with illustrations of dismembered or decapitated fetuses, even if the barbaric nature of abortion is thus revealed. Too much should not be expected from education alone.

Dr. Jack Willkie, of Cincinnati, has said: "The prime job that needs to be done is education. If every citizen knew what we know about fetal development, saw pictures and so on, then abortion would be over and gone." I regret to say I do not agree with him. The reason is that doctors and nurses know all about the fetus but they continue with abortion, either for the money or to be consistent with the logic of their sexual philosophy.

We must admire the courage of those who undertake Operation Rescue (blocking the entrance of abortion clinics) and confront the abortion monster face to face. They risk being arrested and charged with trespass, an offence which in the United States might lead to an imprisonment penalty. There is no doubt that OR campaigners have saved many unborn lives, even though for most of the patients they simply have their operations deferred for a day or two. The main fruit of the OR technique is probably an indirect one. That is, it draws attention to the fact that so many good people feel so intensely about this social injustice, and it heightens the consciousness of the community about the abortion scandal. It is similar to the action of Greenpeace when their ship trespasses into French territorial waters near Tahiti. They do not stop nuclear testing but they draw the attention of the world to what is going on.

For my own part, I am too timid to undertake this form of action and therefore I cannot recommend others to do what I myself would not undertake. It appears that simple picketing of abortion clinics is becoming more accepted than OR. It is less hazardous and almost as effective.

The most recent anti-abortion project, the Life Chain, seems to be even more successful while being safe, non-political and non-denominational. It was started in California by Pastor Royce Dunn, of Yuba City. He decided that the only day for this sort of action was a Sunday, the only time from 2 pm to 3 pm and the primary requirement was to enlist the support of all the churches in the neighborhood.

Men, women and children are involved. They line the streets of busy highways, standing six feet apart, and each one holding up a white placard about 20 inches (50 cm.) square bearing the simple message: ABORTION KILLS BABIES. On the recent Respect Life Sunday in California some 140,000 people took part in various Life Chains, the longest one in a Los Angeles suburb stretching for 13 miles.

Finally, if abortion is basically a diabolical manifestation, the only effective weapon against it is prayer. We can pray either in the privacy of our own home or in public outside the local abortion clinics. This does not infringe the law and it serves as a public witness to the real nature of abortion. In this increasingly secularized society the value of prayer is often overlooked, but it is useful to quote the famous line of Alfred Lord Tennyson (d. 1892) on this theme: "More things are wrought by prayer than this world dreams of." The full text is found in *The Coming of Arthur*. King Arthur was dying and he said:

"If thou shouldst never see my face again,
Pray for my soul. More things are wrought by prayer
Than this world dreams of.
Wherefore, let your voice
Rise like a fountain for me night and day.
For what are men better than sheep or goats
That nourish a blind life within the brain
If, knowing God, they lift not hands of prayer
Both for themselves and for those who call them friend.
For so the whole round earth is every way.
Bound by gold chains about the feet of God."

It is now obvious that the abortion evil will not be overcome finally until there is a spiritual renewal in society. And that is just around the corner. As the old maxim puts it, "Suffering refines the spirit." At the present time almost every family is suffering from some spin-off from the Sexual Revolution, but when people have suffered enough — from hatred of children, from infidelity and marriage breakdown, from rape and murder, from satanism, from AIDS and similar infections, from financial hardship — then they will turn to God for help. And when they do, there will be no more abortion.

It is an age-old principle in medicine that you cannot go against Nature without paying some penalty. Abortion (and all the other sexual anomalies discussed in previous chapters) is the enemy of natural sex, natural pregnancy, natural childbearing, natural family life. This is made obvious in the distress, the hatred, the medical disasters, sometimes death, that it causes. All this serves to confirm the old saying: "Man sometimes forgives; God always forgives; but Nature never forgives."

CHAPTER 6

New Reproductive
Technologies

ON the front page of the daily newspaper — a huge picture of a smiling, pretty mother and a happy father, and a lovely newborn baby (or two, or three, or five . . .). Who could be so churlish as to say it's all wrong? The sentimental presentation is so overwhelming — this courageous young couple, their years of sterility, the brilliance of the scientific techniques, the devotion of the doctors who have made *in vitro* fertilization so successful, the financial sacrifice accepted by all those involved. But while we have a duty and an instinct to welcome any new life into this world, it is still proper to deplore the circumstances of the conception in some of the cases — for example when it results from premarital or extramarital sex, or from rape or incest, or finally from IVF.

When Dr. Patrick Steptoe and Dr. Ralph Edwards produced the first IVF baby, Louise Brown, in 1980, they could not have foreseen the subsequent complexity of the subject or the legislative predicament which so many governments have had to face. These would have been beyond the wisdom of Solomon to solve. But once again the Catholic Church, reflecting her divine origin, has given a clear lead in these modern moral dilemmas and has brought order out of chaos, even at the risk of engendering hysteria, rejection and ill will.

In 1987 the Congregation for the Doctrine of the Faith, with the explicit approval of the Pope, produced *Donum Vitae (The Gift of Life): Instruction on Respect for Human Life in its Origin and on the Dignity of Procreation. Replies to Certain Questions of the Day.* Being presented in formal language, the Instruction is sometimes difficult to read but the main points it made are set out below in more popular form. Its grasp of the medical facts is brilliant; in fact the authors have a much clearer understanding than do most doctors.

INDICATIONS

The main reason for undertaking IVF is to overcome the problem of blockage in the Fallopian tubes which prevents access of the sperms (moving up in the cavity of the uterus) to the ovum (passing down the tube). Why are there so many women with blocked tubes? In many cases no answer can be given. Perhaps there was in the past some mild infection, possibly from appendicitis, or from an accidental miscarriage. But in many other cases the cause lies with the doctors or patients themselves: surgical sterilization, or IUD infection, or pelvic infection resulting from promiscuity, or from induced abortion.

The ingenious concept was to stimulate the ovary to produce more than one egg; to time this event to perfection; to extract the eggs by a laparoscopic operation; to expose the eggs to sperm cells in the laboratory; and, if fertilization occurred, to transfer the embryo (ET) into the uterus at about the 16-cell stage. Several embryos are transferred at one sitting in the hope that at least one of them would implant in the womb.

As time went on it became clear that even patients with patent tubes could, for some unexplained reason, benefit from the IVF technique. Achieving pregnancy for a married couple with tubal blockage came to be known as "the simplest case," and theologians hoped that such an uncomplicated situation would be morally acceptable. Such was not the case. Soon the more bizarre applications of this scientific advance began to surface.

There are numerous permutations and combinations to consider. The sperm might come from the husband, or from a stranger, called a "donor." The ovum might come from the wife, or from a donor. The resulting embryo might be implanted in the uterus of the wife, or of the ovum donor, or of some quite unrelated third woman. The latter two are termed "surrogate" mothers.

Cases have been reported in which a woman has "donated" an ovum to her sterile sister, who went on to be the surrogate mother. The baby she produced was therefore her own nephew, her husband's stepson, and the donor's true child as well as her stepson, too. In an even more ridiculous case, a woman donated an ovum to her own mother. Here the baby was the mother's stepson and grandson at the same time; and the donor's son and half-brother. Is medicine still a "caring" profession?

In all the drama between husband, wife, donors and surrogates, it is easy to overlook the one who is the final end of all this endeavor — the child. At best, he is loved. At worst, he is manipulated, frozen, stored, bought and sold, and sometimes killed. He is the subject of litigation and of legislation. He might expect that the law would protect him but that is rarely the case, not when the doctors want him declared a non-person up to day-14 of pregnancy so that they may experiment on him if they wish. And later in pregnancy they may now abort him if he has any abnormality, or even if he has too many brothers and sisters in the womb at the same time.

The whole thing has become so artificial that it bears little resemblance to ordinary human sex and reproduction. It is bogged down in acronyms: IVF (*in vitro* fertilization); ET (embryo transfer); GIFT (gamete intra-Fallopian transfer); LTOT (low tubal ovum transfer); PROST (pronuclear stage transfer); and other new ones every month.

In Britain the Human Fertilisation and Embryology Bill (1990) gives assent to all these activities and to the refined attacks on the embryo or fetus. Allied to this is such experimental work as "twin fission" (artificial production of twins by dividing the original cells) and cloning; or parthenogenesis (needling the ovum to produce a new being without the intervention of the sperm). There has even been the production of human-animal hybrids by fertilizing an animal ovum with a human sperm. This is the ultimate in the perversion of science. It has been prohibited by law — but the law means nothing to many doctors.

CRYOPRESERVATION

This ingenious discovery (from the Greek, *kruos* = frost) enables the early embryo to be frozen via liquid nitrogen and stored for months or years until a convenient time for implantation and pregnancy. It is amazing that the process is possible with little risk to the developing fetus. The original idea was a clever plan to cope with the multiple ovulations which are stimulated by the initial medications. Usually two or three ova are fertilized and introduced into the womb in the hope that at least one would "take." But why waste any "spare" ova or embryos, as they are called? Freeze them and use them again later. In some cases the widow has been impregnated after her husband has died, which must be the ultimate in the macabre.

As anyone with any common sense could have foretold, the manipulation of frozen embryos could land the doctors in unexpected difficulties. In a notable case in Melbourne, which led the world in this field, several embryos were frozen and stored. The mother and father not long after were both killed in a car accident, and left very large estates. What to do with the unfortunate offspring, living in a state of suspended animation? The case went to court and the judge recommended implantation in a surrogate rather than simple destruction.

In an interesting American case in 1990, a couple produced several embryos which were frozen. They then fell out and had a divorce. Junior (sic) Davis wanted the embryos destroyed while Mrs. Davis said they were hers and she wanted a pregnancy at some later date, a plan that was anathema to Junior.

A judge ruled that the embryos "belonged" to Mrs. Davis, a judgment which unwittingly emphasized the status of the child as an "object" created to satisfy the desires of the parents and then used as a weapon between them. Presumably Junior was very put out about this decision and the prospect that he could in later years be confronted by children whom he had never known. He wished he had never heard of IVF.

This sort of domestic drama should not have surprised those involved because the doctors and clients who go in for IVF do not, as a general rule, have an elevated and refined philosophy of marriage and sexuality. The doctors have no hesitation about producing offspring for those in "stable" *de facto* situations and even for lesbians. The whole point of *de facto* unions is that they are unstable, that is, the partners may separate whenever they wish. And that is exactly what the majority do, to the disadvantage of the woman and the children.

Producing pregnancies for lesbians serves only to confirm them in their perversion and in their hatred for men. The pathetic children produced in these anomalous social unions, both lesbian and *de facto*, are robbed of their ordinary human right to have two parents and to be brought forth within the warm protection of a normal marriage. Has the medical profession the right to produce illegitimates?

SURROGACY

This is a relatively new word in the medical vocabulary, although it has had a long association with the law and the church. It might have been simpler to have kept to its synonym, "substitute" but the Latin (from *rogare*, to ask) sounds more professional and respectable. IVF mas introduced the practice of using surrogate mothers in whose "wombs for rent," as they are called, the babies produced in the laboratories are implanted.

During 1989 the IVF *cause célèbre* involving Mary Beth Whitehead and her baby, Melissa, was finally decided on appeal in the Supreme Court. In answer to an advertisement asking for help to infertile couples, Mrs. Whitehead agreed to artificial insemination with the spermatozoa of Bill Stern. She discovered later that Betsy Stern did not have a sterility problem; she was a career woman who did not want to take time out to cope with a pregnancy and delivery.

When Melissa was born Mrs. Whitehead realized that the child's genetic material was partly derived from her and she refused to part with the baby. As she said, if she accepted the $13,000 promised that would be the price for which she would have sold her baby. After months of legal wrangling, the baby was awarded to the Sterns and Mrs. Whitehead was given visiting rights.

Nothing could more clearly illustrate the essential evil of IVF and surrogate parenting, which are all part of the same deal. The child is obviously a chattel to be contracted for, sold or disputed in court. Mr. Stern was in error by producing semen by masturbation and then allowing it to be introduced into a third party. The surrogate mother was at fault through receiving it. Mrs. Stern and Mr. Whitehead connived in this infringment of the exclusive nature of marriage.

If any or all of the four actors in this unfortunate human drama had

had any religious appreciation of God's plan for sexuality and marriage, these tragic events would not have occurred. The old term, "Holy Mother Church," explains how she protects her children from harm and stupidity.

There have now been several disputes similar to the Whitehead case, and some governments have moved to outlaw the practice. It seems remarkable that doctors should have the freedom to embark on this sort of clinical experiment, create new human beings through IVF, implant them wherever they wish, or perform sex change operations and ultimately oblige Parliament or Congress at enormous expenditure of time and money to legislate to control or prohibit their activities. There is even an animal form of surrogacy — the implanting of a human embryo within the uterus of an animal. It would, of course, be impossible for the pregnancy to proceed very far but it enables the mad scientists to do some experiments. This is the ultimate in the degradation of a human being.

It can be done in animal husbandry so why not in humans? Valuable cattle embryos have been produced by artificial insemination and then transferred into the uteri of rabbits for ease of transporting overseas. The gynecologists are desperate to keep up with the vets.

Similar strictures must apply to the use of an artificial "uterus" in the laboratory; this merely keeps the embryo alive for a short while and allows for experimentation. Space age scientists predict that it should be possible to perfect a device which would allow the baby to develop for months in the laboratory. Whatever the intentions of the doctors involved, this is an insult to human dignity. It is reminiscent of the publicity given to Dr. Lawrence Lawn, of Cambridge, who in the early 1980s was photographed alongside a fluid medium bath in which he was keeping a decapitated fetal head alive, perfused with saline and oxygen. The biblical phrase, "having a heart of stone," could be applied to modern doctors.

MULTIPLE PREGNANCIES

These are an unavoidable feature in IVF work. It is difficult to stimulate only a single ovulation, but in fact there is some advantage in having several embryos to implant because not all of them will survive. Not infrequently the mother finds herself pregnant with quadruplets, quintuplets, sextuplets, etc. This is more than she bargained for. She could cope with two babies, or possibly three, but larger numbers would be an insuperable social and financial burden. What to do?

Simply ask your obliging and resourceful doctor. He has a vested interest in the matter, too, even if he does not mention it to the patient. If he leaves the pregnancy undisturbed, the patient must face weeks of hospitalization before the delivery, the babies will certainly be premature, and they will need perhaps three months of postnatal pediatric care. All of this might add up to a million dollars! Who does the patient sue for this huge sum but her friendly doctor? It is obviously in everyone's interests to remedy the situation.

This is done by the brilliant new technique of "selective reduction of pregnancies." Under ultrasonic scan control when the babies are about 20 weeks or larger, the doctors pierce each one through the heart with a long needle attached to a syringe and then inject some KCi (potassium chloride) which stops the heart beating. In scientific language this is described as "creates asystole," but in ordinary terms it means "kills it." When they reduce the living babies to a manageable number, usually two (twins), they abandon their "search and destroy" mission. Of course, if the customer (patient) say she wants only one baby, thank you, they will obligingly eliminate one of the remaining twins.

In 1990 Dr. R.J. Wapner and seven colleagues (to share the fame, or the responsibility, or guilt) reported that they had managed 46 pregnancies in this way in a Philadelphia hospital. There were about 230 fetuses at the beginning, and when they had finished there were 75 live babies. This was 94 percent of the fetuses which had been spared the potassium chloride. Three of the fetuses had refused to die and had to have a second go with the needle. The authors concluded that "Selective reduction of multifetal pregnancies . . . is an ethically justifiable option." Comment is superfluous.[1]

Despite their romantic image as wonderworkers who produce babies for apparently hopeless cases of sterility, the fact still remains

---

1. Wapner, R.J. "Selective reduction of multifetal pregnancies." *Lancet* (1990), *335*, 90-93.

that the vast majority of IVF practitioners are also abortionists. This is a curious anomaly, a contradiction in terms, but its recognition is very important. Apart from the horrors of "selective reduction of pregnancies," most IVF clinics require their patients when they register to agree in writing to amniocentesis or an ultrasound scan during the middle trimester and, if an abnormality is diagnosed, to an induced abortion. This is an implicit acknowledgment of the increased risk of abnormality when the pregnancy is artificially interfered with at an early stage. Moreover, the sexual philosophy of both doctors and patients involved in this work lends itself to acceptance of abortion. At the same time, one must admire the overall determination of all involved to produce a baby and bring a new and innocent life into the world.

MORAL ASSESSMENT

When one sees the happiness of motherhood for a sterile couple and the remarkable success of the IVF complex procedures, it seems ungracious to raise the question of morality. But the truth must be faced, and if these activities are ethically wrong they must be harmful to all involved and to society. Considering the elements required for a moral assessment, there is no doubt that the *intention* is good; the *circumstances* are unexceptionable; but the *act* (what is done) is in the great majority of cases wrong. This is, of course, an unpopular stance to adopt — but the Church, almost alone, has the courage to do its duty in the area of moral teaching.

The fundamental error in IVF is that it separates the loving nature of sex from its fertile nature. This is the same error that makes masturbation, contraception, sterilization and homosexuality unacceptable. As the instruction, *Donum Vitae*, points out, this teaching was expressed in the famous encyclical, *Humanae Vitae* (1968) which rocked the world by stating that contraception was still immoral and always would be. (As the translation is not always felicitous, I add my own suggestions in brackets.) In it Pope Paul VI stated:

"The teaching [that each and every marriage act must remain open to the transmission of life — even though it rarely achieves it], often set forth by the Magisterium, is founded upon the *inseparable connection,* willed by God and unable to be broken by man on his own initiative, between the two meanings [aspects] of the conjugal act: the unitive [loving] meaning and the procreative [fertile] meaning.

"Indeed, by its intimate structure, the conjugal act [intercourse], while most closely uniting husband and wife, capacitates them for the generation of new lives [enables them to generate new lives], according to laws inscribed in the very being of man and of woman.

"By safeguarding both these essential aspects, the unitive [loving] and the procreative, the conjugal act preserves in its fullness the sense of true mutual love and its ordination [orientation] towards man's most high [noble] calling of parenthood. We believe that the men of our day are particularly capable of seizing [understanding] the deeply reasonable and human character of this fundamental principles." (n. 12)

While this may at first sight appear to be an artificial analysis of the issue, its importance is highlighted in the case of an IVF couple when the wife is having an ovum (or ova) "harvested" in the hospital while the husband, a hundred miles away on a business trip, produces the semen and sends it home by courier. This is the ultimate in the separation of sex from love, and is obviously a travesty of marriage. But the same difficulty exists in every IVF procedure, although in a less dramatic form.

It is obvious, therefore, that for human beings the only licit manner of transferring the germ cells between husband and wife is within the context of the loving marital embrace.

But all is not lost. There are a few acceptable IVF techniques which preserve normal intercourse and achieve fertilization not in a laboratory dish but within the uterus of the wife. These are mainly of the LTOT or GIFT type, but the details of the procedures would have to be spelled out. There could be no objection to harvesting the ova by laparoscopy and then transferring them into the uterus or proximal tube, where they would be accessible to intravaginal ejaculation of semen. It is impossible to observe fertilization by this method, but it is sometimes successful and it seems to be gaining in acceptance.

SECONDARY FAULTS

In nearly every case the semen is obtained by masturbation, which is always unacceptable. With exquisite vulgarity the local IVF clinic calls the special masturbation room "the semenary." The room is furnished with pornographic magazines to stimulate the morally insensitive husband to perform. Not one of medicine's most noble services to the patients.

Those who go in for IVF have, in general, little respect for the life and the dignity of the embryo. This is shown by their willingness to consider abortion if there is any abnormality; by encouraging experimentation on the fetus; by commercial trafficking in organs for transplant; by producing "spare" embryos which are frozen and stored. All these activities, as well as producing animal-human hybrids, are illicit.

By a strange paradox IVF has become one of the most insidious attacks on the dignity and integrity of marriage. This state, ordained by God, is an exclusive relationship between husband and wife, not simply in physical sexual intercourse but also in the mutual giving of genetic material from one partner to the other via the germ cells. These considerations are thoughtlessly rejected by IVF practitioners when they offer their services to those who are not married (*de factos* or lesbians), or when they introduce spermatozoa or ova from third party "donors." This involves a technical form of adultery.

Using surrogate mothers is also illicit. Not only does it offend against the esthetic concept of childbearing, it also is morally wrong because it harms the dignity and the unity of procreation.

Finally IVF is an insult to the child. Even though the parents are loving and courageous, the child becomes an object, an achievement. There are already many cases where the promised happiness does not eventuate and, through human weakness, he is later abandoned or his custody is fought over in the courts. Every child has the right to know that he was conceived in love from parents who were married and committed to each other for life. When he eventually comes to know that he was conceived in the local laboratory, thanks to the kind services of a mad medical scientist, or that his donor father or mother is completely unknown, having been paid off several years before for a single "service," he may become psychologically disturbed.

The child is a gift from the Creator, hence the accuracy of the term "procreation." As Pope Pius XII has pointed out, when two people marry they have a right to intercourse but not necessarily to fertility, to a child. If that were so, sterility would be grounds for annulment. Not having fertility as a natural right, the partners cannot claim that they can go to any lengths to produce a child. They may use only licit means to improve their initial fertility endowment.

CLINICAL RESULTS

The adulation poured out on IVF by the popular press and the admiration for the scientific ingenuity of its techniques both obscure the fact that these reactions are not universal. For a while the Catholic Church was cast in the role of The Spectre at the Feast, but now there is a rising tide of criticism from many quarters.

One of the most incisive commentators is a woman, Renate Klein, whose book's subtitle ("Women speak out about their experiences of reproductive medicine") was more informative than its title.[2] The complaints of her women contributors from several countries were filled with bitterness and disappointment. They all had bad experiences at the hands of IVF doctors, painful procedures, dangerous reactions to the superovulation stimulating drugs, excessive expense and poor final results.

The ladies have formed their own organization of distressed infertile members, called FINRRAGE (Feminist International Network of Resistance to Reproductive and Genetic Engineering). They believe that ". . . the externalization of conception and gestation facilitates manipulation [of women and babies] and eugenic control." Their reaction will command widespread sympathy.

2. Klein, Renate D. *Infertility*, Pandora, London. 1989.

Support for them comes from an unlikely source, the English medical journal, *The Lancet.*[3] In an anonymous commentary it stated that in an American survey of IVF clinics, *half* of them had never sent a woman home with a live baby! This was in 1985, and undoubtedly techniques have improved a little since then — but still the majority of the clients must end up disappointed. The live birth incidence in several American and British clinics was less than 10 percent! And because of the increased incidence of prematures and abnormality, the uncomplicated live births numbered only 5 percent. They pointed out the harm to the women from hormone use, psychological stress, the operations and the anesthetics.

In the *Medical Journal of Australia* (1988) there was a leading article[4] and a special article[5] on this subject, both quoting depressing results from IVF. The latter was one of the most comprehensive reports up to date, being a combined study from all the IVF clinics in Australia and New Zealand. There were 1510 pregnancies, of which only 57.5 percent resulted in a live birth. This was because of the high incidence of ectopics (5% - round figures only), of spontaneous miscarraiges (24%), of multiple pregnancies (22%), or prematures (27%), and of mature but low birth-weight babies (35%).

The perinatal death rate (stillbirths plus neonatal deaths) was very high — 48 per 1000 births, which is about five times the national average.

The leading article commentary (note its melancholy title) pointed out that the report above did not provide an accurate picture because it was based not on all the initial patients who came to the clinics but only on those, a small minority, who subsequently became pregnant. An earlier report in 1986 stated that of 1923 patients registering, only 15% became pregnant. The overall cost per baby was almost $15,000.

Considering the radical nature of the interference during early pregnancy (extracting the ovum from its natural environment; storage

3. "IVF: on the receiving end." *Lancet.* Notes and Views. (1989), Aug. 5, *2*, 342.
4. Stanley, F.J. "In-vitro fertilization — a gift for the infertile or a cycle of despair?" *Med. J. Aust.* (1988), *148*, 425-6.
5. "Australian IVF Collaborative Group." *Med. J. Aust.* (1988), *148*, 429-36.

of the spermatozoa; fertilization in a laboratory dish instead of within the tube; transfer of the embryo into the uterus; freezing and thawing of the cryopreserved embryo) and the drugs used in stimulating ovulation, etc., it is not surprising to find that congenital abnormalities were increased. There is no record of the babies which were diagnosed in time and aborted, but in the 1986 series the incidence of neural tube defect (spina bifida or anencephally) was increased five-fold, and cardiac defects (especially transposition of the great vessels) six-fold among those which came to birth.

There were other important facts which were not mentioned by either of the above authors. Two of the mothers died, presumably from anesthetic or operative complications. As they had been accepted as clients, they presumably were normal healthy women. Of all the embryos produced by IVF, 96% were lost! And of those which advanced far enough to be frozen and stored, the loss rate was 50%.

The conclusion must therefore be that it is always dangerous to reject the law of God, especially in reproduction. Any benefits promised prove to be illusory or bought at too high a risk. It is better to accept the cross of infertility than to go to any lengths to remedy matters. Even if the IVF is achieved by licit procedures, there are still many obstetric hazards which will be almost impossible to eliminate. And the fees charged are unconscionable.

CHAPTER 7

Sterility and Artificial Insemination

STERILITY is one of the saddest things to afflict a marriage, even in our society which has largely turned its face against childbearing. The deep elemental desire to have children, to leave our mark on history in our own small way, to project our eternal selves into the future, is an instinct that is difficult to extinguish.

It sometimes seems paradoxical when a gynecologist may have on his operating list one case for abortion; the next in which he is trying to preserve a pregnancy (say, by a Shirodkhar suture around the cervix); another to be sterilized; and the last a complicated procedure to reopen tubes which he himself might have destroyed some time in the past.

On the other hand, provided that only licit procedures are employed, it is quite proper for the doctor to seek to improve fertility in some cases and to damp it down in others. It is unfashionable to use the term "sterility"; the preferred one is "infertility," which is thought to be more acceptable to the patient but it is largely a matter of semantics. As far as the patient is concerned, she can't get pregnant and she wants something done about it — if possible.

CAUSES OF STERILITY

In the woman, the commonest problem is tubal obstruction, a condition of which she may be quite unaware because there are no leading symptoms. Apart from cases who have had a surgical sterilization, the usual cause of obstructed tubes is infection of one sort or another. Appendicitis and peritonitis may block the outer opening of the tubes; or the inside cavity may be gummed up by venereal infection (a constant risk of promiscuity), or from an IUD, or after a miscarriage, especially if it was surgically induced.

The reproductive mechanism is so complex that there are innumerable reasons for it to break down, many of them too obscure to be diagnosed; indeed it is almost a miracle that it performs so well most of the time. But other causes might be: ovarian cysts; endometriosis; failure of the pituitary gland hormones; partial or complete absence of menstruation; ovarian failure; atrophy of the endometrium (within the uterus), either because of age or from prolonged use of "the pill"; "hostile" mucus in the cervix; and so on.

In the male, a few cases have a problem of impotence. But the majority have normal potency and the semen can be deposited at the vault of the vagina. The common fault is that the semen contains few spermatozoa, or in some cases none at all. In most cases this is a mysterious failure of function of the sperm-forming cells; in a few it is the obvious result of a previous sterilizing operation (vasectomy); and in another small group it is the result of mumps in adolescence.

When I was in the Navy we had a devastating epidemic of mumps aboard my ship, which had a complement of 850 men. About one quarter of them suffered from the infection over the course of about a month, and of those about 20 percent developed infection of one or both testicles (orchitis). I often wondered how many of them would be sterile in later years. We were in action much of this time and we were almost on the point of having to withdraw from the Fleet, but the epidemic suddenly waned and we were able to fight on.

INVESTIGATION

Investigating the wife presents no moral problems. It is not difficult to make sure that ovulation is occurring, that the hormone secretion of pituitary and ovaries is normal, that the cervix is healthy, and that the tubes are either patent or blocked.

A common mistake is to rush into investigation too soon, and in these days of active intervention this sometimes means unnecessary operations. Even if the gynecologist considers that the couple have not allowed enough time for Nature to achieve a pregnancy, he may respond to the impatient demands of the wife. This is often the case with the woman who has been "on the pill" for several years, then discontinues taking it and expects to become pregnant in two or three months. She says, "Look, I'm getting older, I haven't time to wait for your arbitrary one or two years." You should have thought about that before, the doctor thinks, but he is bulldozed into active management and she conceives the baby which would probably have come along without all the stress and pain and expense of medical care. But the doctor takes the credit and the credit card as well.

Of course, if there is any obvious problem such as difficulty with penetration, or infrequent periods, or previous bilateral orchitis, there is no point in delaying investigation. But if everything seems to be going along normally, the couple should wait for at least one year, or preferably two. By that time about 80 percent of couples should have conceived. Some couples manage to have only one or two babies during their whole fertile years, even if all the medical tests prove to be normal.

Obviously the husband should be investigated first, because it is simple to eliminate him. There is no point in undertaking complicated investigations in the wife if he has little or no fertility, but some doctors have an obsession for thoroughness and routines, even if common sense dictates otherwise. For example, I once saw a husband who had had six children but two of them were killed in a car crash. The couple wanted to have another baby but, since she was now in her 40s, the pregnancy was slow in arriving. So off they must go to the all-powerful doctor. He immediately requested a semen specimen "to see if you are fertile"! The evidence of his fertility was all around for everyone to see, not from the laboratory report but from his record of offspring. In men, unless there is some injury or infection such as mumps or gonorrhea, fertility continues virtually unchanged year after year. Not surprisingly, the report came back as "normal." Then she had to be put through the hoops. She eventually conceived.

It must be stressed that the main thrust of sterility work is in investigation. Only about 10 percent of patients can be helped by treatment. The wife can be helped in several ways but, in general, if there is a defect in the husband nothing can be done to remedy things. This is a humbling admission of fact.

The standard practice in the once noble medical profession is to ask the husband to masturbate. Doctors, especially psychiatrists, have been telling themselves and the patients for years that masturbation is "normal" and, if the man feels an instinctive revulsion and guilt in the act, this is immediately attributed to his faulty religious (Catholic, of course) upbringing.

This attitude fails to explain why masturbation, while probably being the commonest sexual fault, has never in the past more honest centuries been accepted as normal. This sexual faculty is obviously designed for use with one of the opposite sex, not in isolation. Therefore it is always morally wrong and no circumstances ever justify it. It must be recognized, of course, that many subjects would not be culpable because of ignorance or (medical) duress.

Besides all this, it is mildly irritating to realize that the masturbation specimen of semen is both unnecessary and, as far as benefit to the patient is concerned, useless. The reason for making this earth-shattering statement is as follows. The report on the semen gives: the volume of the total ejaculate; the density of the sperm cells (number per ml.); total sperm count (density x volume); morphology (percentage of normal and abnormal forms); motility (percentage of sperms moving, which is a very personal assessment); pH (acidity); viscosity; liquefaction; and each laboratory adds a few more esoteric observations as its specialty.

The single most important factor is the sperm density, that is, the number of sperms per ml. A few years ago anything less than 80 million was considered to be oligospermia (too few sperms), but now the normal figure has been dropped to about 20m., which shows how arbitrary the whole examination is.

The main point to be made is that, if any "abnormality" is reported, there is no way it can be influenced by "treatment." If the sperm count is too low, there is no proof that it can be improved by wearing loose underpants (sic), or by having a varicocele (varicose veins in the testicle) operated on, or by having hormone injections. It is impossible to improve the motility, or to alter the pH, the viscosity or anything else — not that they are of the slightest importance in fertility. These factors remain simply interesting laboratory observations.

POST-COITAL SEMINOLOGY

The obvious alternative, which has served well for over 100 years (Marion Sims practiced obstetrics in New York in the middle of the 19th century), is to examine the semen after normal intercourse. The standard procedure has been as follows. The couple are asked to have intercourse and then come without too much delay to the doctor's office. He takes some of the mucus from the cervix (preferably about the time of ovulation when the fluid is clear and translucent) and places it on a microscope slide for examination.

If good numbers of normal, motile sperms are seen, fertility can be assumed. Motility goes off after an hour or so, but sometimes even a day later moving sperms can be seen. It is obvious that this method does not allow of a precise sperm count, but that is not a matter of practical importance. This historic investigation is called the Sims (or Huhner) test. One of its limitations is that absence or sperms or of motility cannot confidently be taken as evidence of sterility.

In recent years I have abandoned the Sims test, partly because of its lack of precision and also because my habitual laziness appreciates the value of transferring the investigation to the laboratory. I therefore use only the postcoital urethral residue of semen. This provides undiluted semen which is not inactivated by vaginal secretions. In that it involves only normal intercourse, it is ethically and esthetically acceptable to all husbands and wives, and it demonstrates that refinement of taste is not completely lost in the medical profession.

The patient is provided with a microscope slide and the delicate coverglass, and at the end of the normal act the husband drops onto the slide a small amount of semen that remains in the urethra. This is immediately covered with the coverglass and the specimen will remain moist for about three hours. It is taken to the local laboratory and examined without delay. Motility and morphology of the sperms are easy to assess. The sperm count is expressed as: so many per high power field.

A count of, say, 100 per HPF is equivalent roughly to about 100 million per ml. in the masturbation specimen; 50 to 50; 10 to 10. It is therefore possible on the basis of this simple count to classify males into three broad groups: those with high fertility; those with low fertility; and those with apparently no fertility — no sperm cells (azoospermia). But it is prudent practice never to make a diagnosis of "You are quite unable to have a baby," either in the husband or the wife. There are many unexplained surprises in this work, and it does not pay to create a class of patients who rush about claiming a "miracle" pregnancy.

The main aim of seminology, whether by the masturbation method or this more decent procedure, is to sort out patients into the above three groups. Those in the first two (high or low sperm counts) are advised to wait patiently for a pregnancy to occur, while those in the third (very few or no sperms) should adopt without delay, but never giving up hope.

I first publicized the above-mentioned method of semen examination in *The Lancet* in 1959.[1] I had never seen anything like it in the medical literature, but I cannot believe that it had not been tried before. It was taken up by the authors of a standard American textbook of laboratory techniques[2] and therefore it should be known by practitioners working in these fields (infertility and pathology), but regrettably it has been largely ignored by the profession. (Dare one opine that they could not recognize genius when they saw it?) It is difficult to discuss the test objectively with colleagues, but it was reported more fully in the premier journal of medical ethics, the *Linacre Quarterly*.[3]

OBSTETRICAL INVENTIONS

A diversion — Would the reader forgive me if I refer to two of my

1. Dunn, H.P. *Lancet* (1959), Nov. 28, p. 974. Corresp.
2. Davidson, I. and Walls, B.B. *Todd-Standard Clinical Diagnosis by Laboratory Methods.* W.B. Saunders Co., Philadelphia. (1962), p. 926 G.
3. Dunn, H.P. "Semen Examination." *Linacre Quart.* (1989), *56*, 12-15.

other inventions in the obstetrical field which, while not exactly relevant to our subject, are nevertheless interesting, even exciting?

The first was a vaginal speculum to use immediately after delivery to inspect the cervix in cases of persistent bleeding.[4] It is an enormous thing, diameter 3½ inches (9 cm.), large enough to operate through, for example, to stitch up a split in the cervix. It gives a view of the cervix that has never been seen before in the history of the world!

The other was an obstetrical diagram used[5] in teaching students and residents how to interpret the touch-picture they must learn when diagnosing the position and rotation of the baby's head during labor. It is a large flat plastic square with a schematic representation of the pelvic cavity; and on the front of this is a rotating disc in the form of a fetal head. This can be turned to whatever position the head lies in at the time of the vaginal examination. It is an invaluable teaching aid.

ARTIFICIAL INSEMINATION

After the success of this concept in veterinary work, it was almost inevitable that it would be tried in the human animals. In its simplest form, it involves the transfer of the semen of the husband or of another man (the "donor") into the vagina or cervical canal of the wife. The procedure is used when there is sterility (oligospermia or azoospermia) or impotence on the part of the husband. Or sometimes there is an anatomical abnormality which prevents deposition of the semen within the vagina — such as hypospadias (a hole on the under aspect of the penis) or epispadias (a similar defect on the upper aspect).

In the latter cases the procedure is significantly different from the usual. The couple go through the motions of intercourse, the semen ejaculated is lost through the abnormal orifice, is collected as best can be and transferred into the vagina. This is called "assisted insemination"; it is the only licit procedure in this area, but, of course, such defects are very rare.

In all the other cases the standard procedure is for the husband or

4. Dunn, H.P. "New vaginal speculum." *Lancet* (1960), *2*, 1392.
5. Dunn, H.P. "An obstetrical diagram." *Lancet* (1962), *1*, 383.

the donor to produce the semen by masturbation, and the ejaculate is then transferred by syringe into the wife. Sometimes the semen is frozen and used at some more convenient date in the future. Another variation in cases of oligospermia (low sperm count) is for the husband to masturbate repeatedly over several days, the semen is centrifuged in order to concentrate the sperms, and this enriched fluid is later introduced into the wife's generative tract.

In recent years a further development is the use of this procedure in order to help lesbians, or even alleged "virgins," to become pregnant while avoiding any contact with the hated males. The only male involved is the donor who delivers his semen, collects his stud fee, and is never even seen. The ladies do not even need a male doctor. They transfer the semen into the recipient using some simple domestic equipment from the kitchen. This perversion of love and childbearing is regarded as one of the great successes of the Sexual Revolution.

The convention is to call artificial insemination by the husband AIH, and by a donor AID. This makes it sound less sordid.

If Mrs. Smith is going to receive the semen of Mr. Donor Brown, you might wonder why she does not do so in the more efficient and sometimes more enjoyable old-fashioned way instead of through these tortuous medical procedures, but there is an inverted puritanism about sexually liberated patients and doctors. It must be all white coats and asepsis, then there can be no whisper of adultery. That would be improper!

A new and macabre variation of the same theme was the well-publicized insemination of a prominent American lady artist with the frozen sperms of her husband who had died the year before, but had left behind some semen as a sort of going-away gift. This is a fine example of the modern divorce of love from fertility. When one partner is dead, the marriage, along with marital rights and duties, has come to an end. The proper environment for childbearing no longer exists. The resulting child will be permanently disadvantaged. When his father has been dead for 20 years, he will be 18 years old. He will never have known any parent except his mother, but he will gradually become aware of his father's semen production and the artificial nature of his conception. What a legacy!

A similar case was reported in *The Washington Times* of March 13,

1990. A woman in Queens, New York, was suing Idant Laboratories Inc. (the largest sperm bank in the United States), and Advanced Fertility Services, of Manhattan, for doing AIH with the wrong semen. Her husband, who was dying of cancer, had stored some frozen semen as an investment in immortality. In the event, to her chagrin she gave birth to a black baby.

No wonder more and more women are deserting from the Sexual Revolution. Perhaps they have realized, almost too late, that the only true protection for women is to be found within the safe and loving arms of Holy Mother Church.

SEMEN DONORS

What about the *donors?* Organ donors, blood donors and the like are all regarded as heroes of a sort, but AID donors give only their semen. There is the famous project in the United States for certain prominent citizens of Nobel Prize status to give their semen to a bank for the production of future geniuses. One of the donors was 80 years old. "There's no fool like an old fool." It is pathetic to think of all these ageing men masturbating with the spurious aim of passing on their intellectual endowment. There is no certainty that the elite offspring will be anything different from those of the rich and famous whom we know so well — mostly obnoxious and, if not mentally handicapped, often morally handicapped.

The AID entrepreneurs advertise that they enrol only the most desirable donors. Where do they find these paragons of genetic perfection? Is there even one person you meet during the day whom you would choose to be the father of your child? The innate snobbery of the medical profession is revealed in the fact that they commonly choose medical students as donors. As a class they are available, they can be subjected to subtle coercion, and they are usually short of money. For many years the human stud fee stood at $30, which was uncomfortably reminiscent of 30 pieces of silver. Modern inflation has probably raised the price of the life-giving fluid.

The common impression that donors are a less than admirable

species was confirmed by an article in the *Australian Women's Weekly*, July, 1987, which was based on an interview with two of the local donors. One of them stated that he was a chronic masturbator, he enjoyed masturbation and thought to himself that he might as well be paid for doing it, so he enrolled as a donor. He regarded it as a cash-only form of moonlighting, and at the same time he felt he "was doing good for someone." His complaints were that the pornographic magazines which the doctors provided in the masturbation room were usually tattered and were missing the most erotic photos. Why, he asked, did the doctors not get modern and use pornographic videos for their clients? One wonders what sort of children would be produced from perverts like this, but the naive women accept their genetic gifts without demur, or even thought.

The semen is screened for bacterial or viral infection, but this can never be completely excluded. There have been numerous cases of women becoming infected with various venereal diseases, such as gonorrhea. The resulting pelvic infection, usually in the form of salpingitis (inflammation of the tubes), in many cases causes permanent sterility in the wife. At least one case of AID infection from infected semen has been reported. From AID to AIDS in one easy step. This is the ultimate tragedy, but it should not cause any surprise. The old Irish saying goes: "If you sup with the Devil, you need a long spoon." And if you have contact with a group which contains perverts, you are at risk right from the start.

SOCIOLOGICAL IMPLICATIONS

The most serious one is that AID produces large numbers of half-brothers and half-sisters who are unknown to one another. The protagonists dismiss this as a very small concern because, being well diluted in society, they will be unlikely to meet and marry. Even so, the general practice is to limit the number of inseminations from any one donor. In the past he might have been used up to 100 times, but the common restriction now is about 30. Of course, who is to know if the donor, anxious for more easy money, will not go from one infertility clinic to another and run up the maximum donations at each one?

In fact, in any one city the recipients, and probably the donors, will be drawn from a relatively narrow social band. The poor will immediately be excluded because infertility work, especially if associated with IVF, is a very expensive exercise. The rich, because of refinement of taste, would also be partly excluded. Most of the clientele would be drawn from the upper middle class. As it takes about 10 years of marriage to make the fateful diagnosis of male sterility and then to act on it, the age group would be restricted to about 30-40 years. With the servicing restrictions on donors, their employment would also be limited to very few years. Their offspring would therefore all be in a narrow age band, they would live in the same wealthy suburbs and go to similar types of expensive schools. Roman Catholics and other strict religious groups would be automatically excluded.

The AID subculture would therefore be limited to secular humanists in these defined social and financial groups and the chances of intermarriage of their apparent children would not be insignificant. In Los Angeles there was a report of a doctor who had been a semen donor frequently as a medical student and when his own children were teenagers he warned them not to marry anyone from Southern California because it might be a half-brother or half-sister. This was embarrassing and disgusting but at least he was honest and realistic. The perils of permissive sexuality!

LEGAL IMPLICATIONS

While "liberal" doctors blunder on in their exciting and financially rewarding infertility work, the lawyers and legislators are presented with almost insoluble problems to resolve. A common one is the attempt to legitimize the child through falsifying the birth certificate. As he has been conceived through AID it is a lie to list the husband as "father," but the Medical Association has no hesitation in recommending this untruth. The privacy of the donor is regarded as fundamental, and therefore dozens of his children will never know who their father is. This is the reverse of the modern trend in adoption cases to allow the children to trace their fathers (and mothers) and thus know their origins, however unfortunate they may be. But nothing will ever expunge the fact of their illegitimate status. Just another example of the sins of the fathers being visited on their children, which always seems so unfair.

Another legal problem comes to light when, as is not uncommon in secular humanist and sexually permissive circles, divorce is later encountered. The husband decides to discard the child who is not actually his and refuses maintenance. Or there are problems of inheritance, especially if there are other legitimate children. Or he might quote "adultery" with the donor as grounds for the divorce. Or the wife might plead male impotence as grounds for annulment, even though she has borne a child. The human drama is an unending story.

These difficulties were tackled, without much success, by the Feversham Departmental Committee on Human Artificial Insemination (1960) and also by Dame Mary Warnock's Committee on IVF (1987). Neither of them had the courage or insight to recommend legal prohibition of AID or IVF. But the moment of truth was encountered in the Warnock Committee report. They recommended that hereditary titles may not be passed on to the children who resulted from AID or from IVF cases in which the male or female germ cells were not those of the legitimately married titled parents. That means that illegitimate offspring are all right for commoners but not for the nobility. And who could possibly disagree? Meanwhile the liberal and unprincipled medical profession keeps churning out thousands of pathetic illegitimate infants, with no thought for the future.

MORAL ASSESSMENT

While artificial insemination appeals as an ingenious way of helping infertile couples, there is no doubt that the procedure involves actions which are ethically unacceptable. As stated above, the only licit action in this field is "assisted insemination" in the case of a husband who is unable, for a variety of reasons, to deposit the semen within the vagina. In such cases intercourse proceeds naturally, as best the couple can, and then the semen is helped on its way into the reproductive tract.

In all other cases, the first fault is having recourse to masturbation to produce the semen specimen, whether on the part of the husband or the donor. As noted before, this action is wrong in all circumstances and no preceived benefit can justify it.

The major defect is the intrusion of the donor into the marriage. Marriage is an exclusive contract — "forsaking all others" as the marriage ceremony used to say — and this concept does not apply only to physical intercourse, which is what most people inderstand by adultery. It also refers to the genetic material which the partners agree to share in the marriage contract. That is, the children (if any) who are born of their union will take their inherited characteristics only from the two partners and not from any third party, whatever the quality of his motives might be.

AID must therefore be seen as a form of technical adultery. Pope Pius XII spoke on this subject to an International Congress of Catholic Doctors (1949) and pointed out that marriage rights are "exclusive, nontransferable and inalienable." These three adjectives help to clarify the muddled and sentimental thinking that surrounds this subject. "Exclusive" has been dealt with. "Nontransferable" means that the husband may not pass on to a donor his inherent rights and privileges. "Inalienable" implies that no external authority, such as the Government or even the partners themselves may deprive the husband of these rights. The Pope went on to condemn the degraded esthetic nature of AID.

"To reduce the cohabitation of married persons and the conjugal act to a mere organic function for the transmission of the germ of life would be to convert the domestic hearth, sanctuary of the family, into nothing more than a biological laboratory. . . . The conjugal act in its natural structure is a personal action, a simultaneous and immediate cooperation of the spouses which, by the very nature of the agents and the character of the act, expresses the mutual self-giving which, in the words of Holy Scripture, effects the union in one flesh."

Artificial insemination was first condemned by the Church on March 24, 1897, in a Holy Office decree that was approved by Pope Leo XIII.

In 1958 the Archbishop of Westminster made a statement to clarify the situation for the faithful who, at that time, might have been confused by the public debate which led to the formation of the Feversham Committee:

"A man or woman who has part in such degrading practices, committing solitary sin and depriving the artificially produced child of the right to be born in lawful wedlock of husband and wife as Nature demands, grievously frustrates the plan of God."

There it is in a nutshell.

CHAPTER 8

Spirituality in Marriage

PRAYER AND REFINEMENT OF TASTE

WITHOUT an active spiritual life man is simply an animal, of the species *homo sapiens*, or "sap" for short. Furthermore, there is an intrinsic connection between refinement of taste and a healthy prayer life.

Is popular taste really more vulgar than in the recent past? In an amusing interview[1] Hilton Kramer, former art editor and art critic for *The New York Times*, was asked if he considered there was now a vulgarization of culture and absence of beauty. He replied: "There's an absolutely raging and raving vulgarization of American cultural life, everywhere from TV to the local McDonald's to the gift shops in our great museums. It's oceanic in proportion!" Too bad about poor McDonald's!

It is difficult not to agree with Kramer that there is at present an all-enveloping vulgarity of taste in every area of social life, and much of the blame for this must be attributed to innumerable artists and writers, together with the decline in religious practice. In his later years Pablo Picasso revealed how from the 1930s onwards he deliberately embarked on the cult of ugliness, partly because he could see that it would be financially rewarding. At the same time he expressed his contempt for the art critics, the galleries and the purchasing public because they fell for his crude deceptions and knelt adoringly at his feet. Thanks to

---

1. *National Catholic Register*, Nov. 5, 1989.

Picasso and others like him we now have a despairing vulgarity of taste in art, in literature, in common speech, in music and popular songs, in dress and behavior, even in architecture. It is difficult to find a movie or a TV show that does not deluge us in filthy language, repulsive violence, and perverted sexual action.

Refinement of taste must come from the heart, from within, from an emanation of the divine presence in each individual person. Each marriage must aim to make the home an oasis of love, decency and refinement. It is impossible to achieve this happy environment unless it is based on a healthy spiritual life. And this is achieved simply through the unchanging techniques of prayer and penance. The prayer is easy; but the penance part is usually unwelcome.

We can take a lead from the Muslims who, by simply praying to Allah five times daily and by having generous-sized families, are now penetrating into every city in what used to be called Christendom. If we say morning and night prayers and grace with meals, that adds up to five times a day. Add to that the daily Rosary and either Mass or a visit to the Blessed Sacrament, and we are away ahead.

At present Sunday Mass is regarded as the norm, while attendance at Easter and Christmas is the minimal observance. This should be changed to Sunday Mass as the minimal and daily Mass as the norm. If only this were the case, society would be revolutionized. At present in most English-speaking countries, Sunday Mass attendance is down to about 20 percent of the Catholic population. In England, of the total population, Sunday church attendance is only about 10 percent. This indicates an agnostic community.

We do not take readily to communal or public prayer, as we tend to prefer a decent reticence in our relationship with God. However, it is essential that the husband and wife for a start, and any children who may later arrive, should pray together in some form or other. The ideal vehicle is simply morning and night prayers, the Rosary, and occasional Scripture readings. The Rosary takes only 10 minutes. If it is not part of the daily routine, the weeks pass by and no thought is ever given to the great events in the life of Our Lord and of Mary. If these simple recommendations are rejected the family, parents and children alike, will thereby be much more vulnerable to the spiritual menaces which abound in society.

It is commonly recognized that, in the community of love which a marriage is, each partner has an unwritten duty to provide affection, comfort, care and support for the other. It is not so clearly seen that there is a duty also to help each other towards salvation. Every individual has a personal obligation to save his own soul, but in marriage each partner is also partly responsible for the spiritual health of the other. There should therefore be a steady progression in sanctity together. As Our Lord said, this is not too difficult a task. In fact it can be quite pleasant, because His burden is light and His yoke is sweet. (Matthew 11:28-30) From my experience in practice, I knew great numbers of happy marriages which attained to this ideal in an unspectacular way.

ROLES IN MARRIAGE

In the confusion of modern society, it is more important than ever to have a clear perception of the inherent duties of each spouse. One of the great harms that militant feminism has done to vast numbers of good young women is to confuse them about their role, both in the community and within marriage. It is only by keeping close to Nature and to the plan of the Creator that lasting happiness can be attained, and this design is so brilliant that no passing fashion of behavior can change it. The historical origins of humanity and marriage are described in the Bible, both Old Testament and New Testament, and one would have to have a blind self-confidence to reject it all as myth or irrelevant.

Nobody can understand the detail of Creation because the imaginative sweep of the divine plan surpasses anything man's intelligence could conceive of. But there must be some fundamental importance in the simple statement that God created man in His "own image and likeness." Adam was created first, and then there was that touching statement that "it is not good for man to be alone," so God created woman to be his companion and helper. Woman came from man's body, and thereafter all men came from woman's body. Each sex showed itself capable of great good or great evil. The first sin of our noble parents, as for each one of us, was pride — wanting to be like gods, knowing both good and evil. They were tricked by the common fallacy that knowledge of evil is in some way desirable, but since that epic mistake we realize that the less we know about evil the better. Knowledge of good is the only good. From that historic time man has filled the role of protector and provider while woman has been the love-giver, the life-giver, the nurturer, the source of beauty and delight.

The modern mistake is that women are trying to be like men (and to a lesser extent the men like women). They have opted out of life-giving and have gone to war, they have taken up boxing, wrestling, even rugby football. These are not listed in the Bible as signs of the End Times, but that must have been an oversight. When women are tackling others with the ball, it seems like the end of the world.

For guidance in determining the role of husband and wife and their relationship to each other, we must turn to St. Paul who deals with these matters is his epistles, mainly in Ephesians 5:21-33. In these days of women's "liberation" it is fashionable for even good women to denigrate St. Paul and call him a chauvinist, woman-hater, and so on. Such ignorance is often inexcusable. This apostle was one of the greatest intellects in Christian history, he had amazing endurance and courage right up to his martyrdom, and he was favored by God through several dramatic miracles as the special apostle for us Gentiles. What he says should not therefore be dismissed lightly. If we do not care for what he says, the fault lies with us, not with him or his cultural milieu.

The proletarian view is that St. Paul favors husband dominance and the subservience of wives, but it should be obvious from the text of the above reference that he stresses equality in almost every circumstance. It is actually insulting to this great saint to make him the butt of such smallminded criticism, but it would be useful here to quote the full controversial section from Ephesians:

"Wives, be subject to your husband, as to the Lord. For the husband is the head of the wife as Christ is the head of the church, his body, and is himself its Savior. As the church is subject to Christ, so let wives be subject in everything to their husbands.

"Husbands, love your wives, as Christ loved the church and gave himself up for her, that he might sanctify her, having cleansed her by the washing of water with the word, that he might present the church to himself in splendor, without spot or wrinkle or any such thing, that she might be holy and without blemish. Even so husbands should love their wives as their own bodies. He who loves his wife loves himself. For no man ever hates his own flesh, but nourishes and cherishes it, as Christ does the church, because we are members of his body. 'For this reason a man shall leave his father and mother and be joined to his wife, and the two shall become one.' This is a great mystery, and I mean in reference to Christ and the church; however, let each one of you love his wife as himself, and let the wife see that she respects her husband."

What benefits do wives get from this admonition? Unconditional love from their husbands. Being compared to the church, which is the object of Christ's love. Receiving the greatest love of which a man is capable (that is, for his own body). Being transformed into something in splendor, holy and unblemished. Being swept up in this great mystery, in which two become one, not only in bodily function but also in mind and heart and spirit. By contrast, the remarks to husbands refer only to authority. Would anyone not prefer an assurance of love?

There can be only one captain on any ship and his authority, like that of the husband, need be invoked only in a crisis situation or a major policy problem. In practice, most marriages sail along smoothly year after year with never a mention of authority or any serious conflict of interest, but the advent of Women's Lib. and working mothers on a grand scale might cause some otherwise avoiable disputes. In these situations someone has to make a decision and, according to St. Paul, it should be the husband.

A marriage in which the partners and children pray together will be so blest with love that these irreconcilable difficulties will never arise. *Amor omnia vincit.* (Love conquers all.)

THE HOLY FAMILY

The ideal for family life usually presented to lay people by the Church is the Holy Family, but the interesting paradox is that sexuality did not feature in the lives of its three members. This confirms the age-old conviction that, for those in the front line of the battle for the Kingdom of God, celibacy is the only way of life because it is essential for them to be detached from the things of this world. The Blessed Virgin can then act as the model for all women, married or unmarried. (Another role model for the young is Rebecca, who was described in Genesis as "a virgin most beautiful, fair of face and no man had touched her."[24:16]) Mary's full title has been from the earliest days "Mary, ever virgin."

A common error held by many of our Protestant friends is that Mary had other children ("brothers and sisters") after Jesus. This would make her only a part-time virgin, after which she settled down to be an ordinary Jewish *hausfrau*. This is an unintentional insult to the Blessed Virgin, whose apostolate continued after the death of her Son. The absence of any other children can be deduced from the unique nature of her relationship to Jesus; from His giving her into the care of St. John while on the cross; and from the absence in history of any men and women who would have been able to claim that "I am a half-brother or half-sister to God!" Remember that the divinity of Christ was well established by the time of the Resurrection, or, for even the most obtuse disciples, by Pentecost.

Apart from these considerations, the members of the Holy Family suffered all the stresses and dramas from which no modern family is immune. Our Lord was abandoned by His closest friends when He most needed them. Nobody has ever experienced torture as He did, so intense that it killed a healthy young man within about 20 hours. He even seems to have known despair when on the cross He cried out, "My, God, my God, why have You forsaken me?" Or was that merely His praying of Psalm 22? Or both?

Mary suffered being pregnant before marriage, even if the conception was miraculous. Soon after her delivery she had to flee in the middle of the night from Herod's irrational hatred of the innocent child, which presaged the modern campaign of abortion, the new Slaughter of the Innocents. Later she lost her darling boy. And in the end she had to watch Him being murdered before her eyes.

St. Joseph suffered everything in silence. He has always been known as "the Just Man," the paradigmatic strong, silent man. But what a happy life he must have had in spite of their necessary poverty, waking up each morning to see this beautiful mother and her delightful Son.

When He was lost at the age of 12 and found again in the temple (where we should always look for Him), his father probably said,

"Mary, darling, don't scold Him! Did you hear Him speaking to the rabbis? That boy's a genius, a saint. But you've always known that, haven't you."

"Joseph, dear, I don't want Him to get too proud. . . ."

Did he ever say to himself with a smile, "That's my boy!"? Of course he did, just like all fathers. Well, perhaps he did. . . .